# PowerShell SysAdmin Crash Course

CW01202948

*Unlock the Full Potential of PowerShell with Advanced Techniques, Automation, Configuration Management and Integration*

*Steeve Lee*

Copyright © 2023 by GitforGits.

All rights reserved. This book is protected under copyright laws and no part of it may be reproduced or transmitted in any form or by any means, electronic or mechanical, including photocopying, recording, or by any information storage and retrieval system, without the prior written permission of the publisher. Any unauthorized reproduction, distribution, or transmission of this work may result in civil and criminal penalties and will be dealt with in the respective jurisdiction at anywhere in India, in accordance with the applicable copyright laws.

Published by: GitforGits
Publisher: Sonal Dhandre
www.gitforgits.com
support@gitforgits.com

Printed in India

First Printing: March 2023

ISBN: 978-8119177042

Cover Design by: Kitten Publishing

For permission to use material from this book, please contact GitforGits at support@GitforGits.com.

# Content

# Preface

"PowerShell SysAdmin Crash Course" is the ultimate guide for system administrators and PowerShell users. This comprehensive resource teaches readers everything they need to know about PowerShell, from the console and cmdlets to scripting, modules, and more.

With hands-on experience and over 50 examples and demonstrations, readers will build a strong understanding of PowerShell and gain confidence in its application. They will also learn essential topics like Active Directory Management, PowerShell Remoting, DSC, SCCM, and administering software updates.

In addition, readers will discover advanced techniques such as working with JSON and XML data, parallel processing, multithreading, and creating custom cmdlets and modules. They will also learn how to integrate PowerShell with automation and configuration management tools like Ansible, Puppet, and Chef, and how to use CI/CD tools like Jenkins. The book also covers integrating PowerShell with Bash and Python scripting and utilizing PowerShell Universal for running automation scripts through a single platform.

In this book you will learn how to:

- Learn everything about PowerShell, from console to cmdlets to scripting and modules.
- Manage Active Directory, PowerShell Remoting, DSC, SCCM, and software updates.
- Discover advanced techniques like JSON and XML data, parallel processing, and multithreading.
- Create custom cmdlets and modules for automation and configuration management.
- Integrate PowerShell with Ansible, Puppet, Chef, Jenkins, Bash, and Python scripting.
- Use PowerShell Universal to run automation scripts through a single platform.

Say goodbye to complicated IT tasks and embrace efficient system administration with "PowerShell SysAdmin Crash Course." Take control of your PowerShell skills and start learning today!

# GitforGits

## Prerequisites

This book is ideal for those who want to build a strong understanding of PowerShell and its application, from the basics to advanced techniques. It is also suitable for those who want to integrate PowerShell with automation and configuration management tools and other scripting languages.

## Codes Usage

Are you in need of some helpful code examples to assist you in your programming and documentation? Look no further! Our book offers a wealth of supplemental material, including code examples and exercises.

Not only is this book here to aid you in getting your job done, but you have our permission to use the example code in your programs and documentation. However, please note that if you are reproducing a significant portion of the code, we do require you to contact us for permission.

But don't worry, using several chunks of code from this book in your program or answering a question by citing our book and quoting example code does not require permission. But if you do choose to give credit, an attribution typically includes the title, author, publisher, and ISBN. For example, "PowerShell SysAdmin Crash Course by Steeve Lee".

If you are unsure whether your intended use of the code examples falls under fair use or the permissions outlined above, please do not hesitate to reach out to us at kittenpub.kdp@gmail.com.

We are happy to assist and clarify any concerns.

# Acknowledgement

I owe a tremendous debt of gratitude to GitforGits, my editor, for their unflagging enthusiasm and wise counsel throughout the entire process of writing this book. Their knowledge and careful editing helped make sure the piece was useful for people of all reading levels and comprehension skills. In addition, I'd like to thank everyone involved in the publishing process for their efforts in making this book a reality. Their efforts, from copyediting to advertising, made the project what it is today.

Finally, I'd like to express my gratitude to everyone who has shown me unconditional love and encouragement throughout my life. Their support was crucial to the completion of this book. I appreciate your help with this endeavour and your continued interest in my career.

# CHAPTER 1:
# BEGINNING WITH POWERSHELL

# What is PowerShell?

PowerShell is a command-line shell and scripting language developed by Microsoft for Windows, Linux, and macOS. It provides a flexible and powerful toolset for automating administrative tasks and managing system configurations, making it a popular choice for system administrators, IT professionals, and developers. PowerShell is built on the .NET Framework (for Windows PowerShell) and .NET Core (for PowerShell Core), which provides access to a rich set of system management tools and APIs. This allows PowerShell to interact with a wide range of system components, including the Windows Registry, Active Directory, and various network services.

One of the key benefits of PowerShell is its rich set of built-in cmdlets. Cmdlets are lightweight, self-contained commands that can be used to perform specific tasks, such as managing files and folders, configuring network settings, and interacting with remote systems. PowerShell includes over 600 built-in cmdlets, covering a wide range of system management tasks. PowerShell also supports the use of modules, which are collections of cmdlets that are designed to work together to accomplish specific tasks. Microsoft provides a number of built-in modules for managing various aspects of the system, such as the Active Directory module for managing users and groups, and the Server Manager module for managing servers and server roles. PowerShell also supports the creation of custom cmdlets and modules, allowing administrators and developers to extend its functionality to meet their specific needs. This makes PowerShell a highly customizable tool that can be tailored to the needs of individual organizations.

## Role of PowerShell

The primary role of PowerShell is to provide an efficient, flexible, and extensible way for IT professionals to manage and automate tasks related to system administration, configuration, and maintenance. This includes managing operating systems, applications, and services, interacting with APIs, working with databases, managing the network, and more. PowerShell also allows administrators to perform tasks across multiple systems, both locally and remotely, thus increasing productivity and reducing the need for manual intervention.

## Features of PowerShell

### *Object-oriented*
PowerShell is an object-oriented scripting language that deals with objects rather than text streams. This means that cmdlets and functions work with structured data, making it easier to process, filter, and manipulate information. This also makes PowerShell highly

extensible, as users can create custom objects, cmdlets, and modules.

## Cmdlets
Cmdlets are specialized .NET classes that perform specific actions and can be used individually or combined to create more complex scripts and workflows. Cmdlets follow a verb-noun naming convention (e.g., Get-Process, Set-Item) that makes them easy to discover and use. There are hundreds of built-in cmdlets in PowerShell, and users can create custom cmdlets to meet specific needs.

## Pipeline
PowerShell's pipeline feature allows users to pass the output of one cmdlet or function as input to another, enabling efficient and powerful data processing. By using the pipeline, IT professionals can perform complex tasks with a single command by chaining cmdlets together.

## Scripting
PowerShell's scripting capabilities allow users to create reusable scripts and functions to automate tasks, manage configuration, and perform complex operations. Script files have a .ps1 extension and can include variables, loops, conditional statements, error handling, and other programming constructs.

## Modules
PowerShell supports modularization through the use of modules, which are collections of cmdlets, functions, and other resources that can be imported and shared. This promotes code reusability and makes it easy to organize and distribute functionality. There are many built-in and community-contributed modules available for various tasks and technologies.

## Remoting
PowerShell Remoting enables IT professionals to execute commands on remote computers and manage multiple systems from a single console. This is achieved through the use of Windows Remote Management (WinRM) protocol or SSH for cross-platform scenarios. Remoting also supports persistent sessions, allowing users to maintain connections and perform multiple tasks without reconnecting.

## Desired State Configuration (DSC)
DSC is a declarative management system in PowerShell that allows administrators to define the desired state of their systems and enforce it through configuration scripts. This ensures consistency and reduces configuration drift, making it easier to maintain and troubleshoot systems.

## Extensibility

PowerShell is highly extensible, as users can create custom cmdlets, functions, modules, and scripts using .NET Framework, .NET Core, and other programming languages such as C#, VB.NET, and Python. PowerShell also provides a rich set of APIs for interacting with various services and platforms, making it an ideal tool for automation and integration.

## Cross-platform support

With the release of PowerShell Core, PowerShell is now available on multiple platforms, including Windows, Linux, and macOS. This enables IT professionals to use PowerShell for managing and automating tasks across heterogeneous environments.

## Security

PowerShell includes several security features, such as execution policies, constrained language mode, and Just Enough Administration (JEA), that enable administrators to manage and secure their systems effectively. PowerShell also integrates with Active Directory and other authentication systems to provide secure access control.

PowerShell's object-oriented approach, built-in cmdlets, pipeline, scripting capabilities, modules, remoting, DSC, extensibility, cross-platform support, and security features make it a valuable asset for IT professionals looking to improve their productivity, efficiency, and control. This eliminates the need for using different tools and scripts for managing different systems and services. With PowerShell, IT professionals can use a single set of commands and scripts to automate tasks, manage configurations, and troubleshoot issues.

# Benefits of PowerShell

One of the key benefits of PowerShell is its ease of use. PowerShell's intuitive syntax and consistent naming convention make it easy to learn and use. The built-in help system and online resources also provide comprehensive documentation and examples, enabling users to quickly get up to speed with PowerShell.

Another benefit of PowerShell is its versatility. PowerShell can be used for a wide range of tasks, from simple one-liners to complex workflows and integrations. PowerShell's extensibility also makes it easy to add custom functionality and integrate with other tools and systems. PowerShell's security features make it a valuable tool for managing and securing systems. PowerShell's execution policies, constrained language mode, and JEA help administrators manage and limit access to systems and data, reducing the risk of unauthorized access and data breaches. PowerShell also provides robust logging and auditing capabilities, making it easy to track and troubleshoot issues. PowerShell logs can be configured to record all executed commands, including their input and output, enabling administrators to quickly identify and address issues.

Its ease of use, versatility, extensibility, security features, and logging capabilities make it a valuable asset to reduce administrator's workload, increase their productivity, and improve the overall performance and security of their managing systems.

# PowerShell vs. Command Prompt

PowerShell and Command Prompt are two powerful tools for managing and automating tasks on Windows systems. Although they share some similarities, there are significant differences between the two tools in terms of features, capabilities, and ease of use. In this section, we'll understand PowerShell in comparison to Command Prompt.

## Data Processing and Output

One of the primary differences between PowerShell and Command Prompt is the way they process and output data. Command Prompt treats all data as text, which can make it difficult to process complex data structures. PowerShell, on the other hand, treats data as objects, which makes it easier to process and manipulate data. PowerShell also includes a powerful pipeline feature, which allows users to chain commands together and process data more efficiently.

## Command Handling

Another difference between PowerShell and Command Prompt is the way they handle commands. Command Prompt uses a limited set of commands and requires users to use external tools to perform more advanced tasks. PowerShell, on the other hand, provides a comprehensive set of built-in cmdlets and modules that allow users to perform a wide range of tasks without using external tools.

## Features and Capabilities

PowerShell provides several features and capabilities that make it a powerful tool for managing and automating tasks on Windows systems. Here are some of the key features of PowerShell:

### Object-oriented scripting language
PowerShell is an object-oriented scripting language that treats data as objects, making it easier to process and manipulate data.

### Built-in cmdlets and modules
PowerShell provides a comprehensive set of built-in cmdlets and modules that allow users to perform a wide range of tasks without using external tools. This includes managing operating systems, applications, and services, interacting with APIs, working with databases, managing the network, and more.

### Pipeline
PowerShell's pipeline feature allows users to pass the output of one cmdlet or function as input to another, enabling efficient and powerful data processing.

### Scripting capabilities
PowerShell's scripting capabilities allow users to create reusable scripts and functions to automate tasks, manage configuration, and perform complex operations.

### Modules
PowerShell supports modularization through the use of modules, which are collections of cmdlets, functions, and other resources that can be imported and shared.

### Remoting
PowerShell Remoting enables IT professionals to execute commands on remote computers and manage multiple systems from a single console.

### Desired State Configuration (DSC)
DSC is a declarative management system in PowerShell that allows administrators to define the desired state of their systems and enforce it through configuration scripts.

Command Prompt, on the other hand, has a limited set of features and capabilities compared to PowerShell. Command Prompt does not support object-oriented scripting, pipelining, or modularization. Command Prompt also does not have a built-in set of cmdlets and modules like PowerShell.

## Ease of Use

PowerShell is generally considered to be more user-friendly and easier to use than Command Prompt. PowerShell's intuitive syntax and consistent naming convention make it easy to learn and use. PowerShell also includes a built-in help system and online resources that provide comprehensive documentation and examples, enabling users to quickly get up to speed with PowerShell.

Command Prompt, on the other hand, has a steeper learning curve and requires users to memorize commands and their syntax. Command Prompt also does not provide a built-in help system or comprehensive documentation.

## Sample Program to Compare Differences

To illustrate the differences between PowerShell and Command Prompt, let us consider a simple task of listing all the files in a directory and their sizes.

### *Using Command Prompt*
- Open Command Prompt
- Navigate to the directory where the files are located using the cd command
- Type the dir command to list all the files in the directory
- Note down the file names and their sizes

### *Using PowerShell*
- Open PowerShell
- Navigate to the directory where the files are located using the cd command
- Type the Get-ChildItem command to list all the files in the directory along with their properties, such as size, name, and type.
- Use the Select-Object cmdlet to select the properties you want to display (in this case, Name and Length)
- Use the Sort-Object cmdlet to sort the files by size

From the above sample illustration, it can be said that the PowerShell commands are more concise and powerful than the Command Prompt commands. PowerShell is also more user-friendly and easier to use than Command Prompt, with a more intuitive syntax and comprehensive documentation.

# PowerShell Editions and Versions

PowerShell has been released in several editions and versions over the years, each with different features and capabilities. Let us take a look at various editions of PowerShell:

## Windows PowerShell

PowerShell is a command-line shell and scripting language developed by Microsoft for system administrators and power users to automate administrative tasks. The original version of PowerShell was released in 2006 as part of Windows Vista and was built on the .NET Framework. It provides a powerful and flexible scripting language with a rich set of built-in cmdlets that can be used to manage various aspects of Windows and other platforms. Due to its popularity and usefulness, Windows PowerShell was later included in

Windows 7, Windows Server 2008 R2, and later versions of Windows. It has since become an essential tool for system administrators and IT professionals who need to automate and manage complex tasks in large-scale environments.

# PowerShell Core

PowerShell Core is a robust and versatile cross-platform scripting language that was introduced in 2016. Based on .NET Core, this version of PowerShell is capable of running on multiple platforms such as Linux, macOS, and Windows. PowerShell Core offers the same language and cmdlets as Windows PowerShell, but with enhanced performance and functionality. This means users can create, manage, and automate their scripts using the same language and tools, regardless of the platform they are working on. With PowerShell Core, developers and IT professionals can streamline their workflow, achieve greater efficiency, and enjoy the benefits of a consistent and reliable scripting experience across all platforms.

# Azure PowerShell

Azure PowerShell is a powerful tool that allows users to manage and automate their Azure environment. With its rich set of cmdlets and modules, users can easily manage various Azure services such as virtual machines, storage, and networking. Azure PowerShell is designed specifically for Azure, making it a reliable and efficient tool for administrators and developers. Its capabilities allow for easy automation of repetitive tasks, improving efficiency and reducing errors. With Azure PowerShell, users can quickly deploy and manage their applications, ensuring they run smoothly and effectively.

# Exchange Server PowerShell

Exchange Server PowerShell is a powerful tool that streamlines managing and automating tasks in Exchange Server. It offers a specialized version of PowerShell with a wide range of cmdlets and modules that enable administrators to efficiently manage Exchange Server components such as mailboxes, distribution groups, and connectors. The cmdlets allow administrators to perform tasks such as creating, modifying, or removing mailbox permissions, managing mailbox databases, and configuring email routing. Additionally, the modules allow administrators to automate processes and create custom scripts to simplify complex tasks.

# SharePoint Server PowerShell

SharePoint Server PowerShell is a specialized version of PowerShell that is tailored to meet the requirements of managing and automating tasks in SharePoint Server. It provides a comprehensive range of cmdlets and modules that are specifically designed to help

SharePoint administrators manage various aspects of SharePoint Server, including sites, lists, and libraries. With SharePoint Server PowerShell, administrators can perform a wide range of tasks, such as creating and deleting sites, managing permissions, configuring site settings, and managing SharePoint workflows. This powerful tool allows administrators to automate repetitive tasks, streamline workflows, and improve the overall efficiency of their SharePoint Server environment.

# PowerShell Versions

Over the years, PowerShell has undergone several updates and versions, each with new features and capabilities. Following is a brief summary I can provide you about the various versions of PowerShell:

## Windows PowerShell 1.0

Windows PowerShell 1.0, the initial release of Microsoft's command-line shell and scripting language, made its debut in 2006 alongside the launch of Windows Vista. It was designed to replace the existing Command Prompt shell with a more powerful and flexible tool for system administrators and power users to automate tasks and manage Windows systems. PowerShell 1.0 laid the foundation for subsequent versions of PowerShell, which have become increasingly popular among IT professionals and developers.

## Windows PowerShell 2.0

Windows PowerShell 2.0 was a significant upgrade released in 2009, as part of Windows 7 and Windows Server 2008 R2. It included several new features and enhancements, such as the PowerShell Integrated Scripting Environment (ISE), which made it easier to develop and debug scripts. Additionally, PowerShell 2.0 introduced remote management capabilities, allowing administrators to manage remote computers and devices from a central console. The support for modules also made it easier to organize and share code between PowerShell users.

## Windows PowerShell 3.0

Windows PowerShell 3.0 was launched in 2012 as a component of Windows 8 and Windows Server 2012. This version brought a range of new functionalities and enhancements to the already powerful automation and scripting tool. With the release of PowerShell 3.0, users gained access to new features, including powerful workflows that can automate complex tasks, a streamlined syntax that made scripting more intuitive and easier to use, and advanced remoting capabilities that enabled IT administrators to manage remote computers more efficiently. These improvements made PowerShell 3.0 an essential tool for IT professionals, enabling them to streamline their work and simplify the management of large-scale IT environments.

# Windows PowerShell 4.0

Windows PowerShell 4.0 was a major release that came out in 2013, bringing with it many new features and enhancements. One of the most notable additions was Desired State Configuration (DSC), which enabled administrators to declaratively specify how they wanted systems to be configured and maintained. PowerShell Web Access was also introduced, allowing users to access PowerShell commands and scripts through a web interface. Additionally, the version included enhanced debugging capabilities, making it easier for users to troubleshoot issues and optimize their PowerShell scripts. Overall, PowerShell 4.0 represented a significant step forward in the evolution of Microsoft's powerful command-line shell and scripting language.

# Windows PowerShell 5.0

Windows PowerShell 5.0 was a major release of Microsoft's command-line shell and scripting language for Windows. It was launched in 2016, and it introduced several new features, including the PowerShell Gallery, which allowed users to easily find and install PowerShell modules and scripts. PowerShell 5.0 also included support for classes, a powerful object-oriented programming feature, as well as new cmdlets that enabled administrators to manage various Windows 10 features more efficiently. With its enhanced capabilities and ease of use, PowerShell 5.0 became a popular tool for automating tasks and managing Windows systems.

# PowerShell 6

Windows PowerShell 6 was a significant milestone for Microsoft, as it marked the first time PowerShell was made available on Linux and macOS in addition to Windows. This cross-platform version of PowerShell included many new features such as improved performance, simplified installation, and expanded support for other operating systems. PowerShell 6 enabled IT professionals and developers to leverage the power of PowerShell on a wider range of platforms, making it easier to manage and automate tasks across their entire IT infrastructure, regardless of the underlying operating system.

# PowerShell 7

Windows PowerShell 7 is the latest version of Microsoft's popular command-line shell and scripting language. Released in 2020, it boasts several new features and improvements over its predecessors, including the ability to run PowerShell Core and Windows PowerShell side-by-side. It also includes new cmdlets that allow for more powerful automation and scripting capabilities, as well as improved compatibility with Azure PowerShell, making it easier to manage resources in the cloud.

From Windows PowerShell to PowerShell Core, Azure PowerShell, Exchange Server PowerShell, and SharePoint Server PowerShell, each edition and versions has been designed to meet the specific needs of IT professionals in managing and automating tasks on various platforms and services.

# Installing PowerShell

Installing PowerShell for the first time on a Windows system is a straightforward process that involves downloading and installing the appropriate version of PowerShell. Here is a step-by-step guide to installing PowerShell on Windows:

## Check Version of Windows

Before installing PowerShell, you should check the version of Windows you are running to ensure compatibility. PowerShell is compatible with Windows 7, Windows Server 2008 R2, and later versions of Windows. You can check your Windows version by going to: Start menu > Settings > System > About.

## Download Appropriate Version of PowerShell

Once you have confirmed the version of Windows you are running, you can download the appropriate version of PowerShell from the Microsoft website. You can download the latest version of PowerShell from the following link:
https://github.com/PowerShell/PowerShell/releases

Scroll down to the section titled "Assets" and download the appropriate version of PowerShell for your system. Choose the MSI installer for Windows systems.

## Run Installer

After downloading the installer, navigate to the location where it was downloaded and double-click on it to run the installer. Click "Yes" when prompted to allow the installer to make changes to your system.

## Accept License Terms

After running the installer, you will be prompted to accept the license terms. Read through the license terms and click "Accept" to proceed with the installation.

## Choose Installation Location

You will be prompted to choose the installation location for PowerShell. By default, PowerShell is installed in the Program Files folder. You can choose a different location if you prefer. Once you have selected the installation location, click "Next" to proceed.

## Choose Installation Type

You will be prompted to choose the installation type. You can choose between a typical installation or a custom installation. A typical installation installs all the necessary components for running PowerShell. A custom installation allows you to choose which components to install. Select the typical installation and click "Next" to proceed.

## Install PowerShell

After selecting the installation type, click "Install" to begin the installation process. The installer will install PowerShell and its required components. This may take a few minutes.

## Launch PowerShell

Once the installation is complete, you can launch PowerShell by clicking the Windows Start button and typing "PowerShell" in the search bar. Click on the PowerShell app to launch it.

## Verify the Installation

To verify that PowerShell is installed correctly, open PowerShell and type "Get-Host" and press Enter. This will display information about the PowerShell version and other details. If PowerShell is installed correctly, this command will display the version of PowerShell you have installed.

In a nutshell, installing PowerShell for the first time on a Windows system is quite a simple process that involves downloading and installing the appropriate version of PowerShell from the Microsoft website. By following the step-by-step guide given above, you can install PowerShell and start using its powerful features and capabilities.

# CHAPTER 2: POWERSHELL BASICS

# Configuring PowerShell Console

PowerShell is a command-line interface (CLI) and scripting language developed by Microsoft for system administrators to manage and automate Windows environments. The PowerShell console provides an interactive environment for running commands, scripts, and modules. It offers a powerful set of features, including pipelining, object-oriented output, and the ability to use .NET Framework and COM objects. PowerShell can also be used to manage remote systems and automate administrative tasks.

To configure the PowerShell console for system administrators, follow these steps:
- Open the PowerShell console by clicking on the Start menu and typing "PowerShell" in the search bar. Click on "Windows PowerShell" to open the console.
- To configure the console settings, right-click on the title bar and select "Properties". This will open the Properties dialog box.
- In the Properties dialog box, you can customize the console appearance by changing the font, size, color, and layout. You can also set the cursor shape and buffer size.
- On the "Options" tab, you can enable or disable various console features, such as QuickEdit mode, Insert mode, and Ctrl key shortcuts. You can also configure the behavior of the function keys and modify the command history settings.
- On the "Layout" tab, you can customize the console window size, position, and buffer size. You can also configure the window title and icon.
- On the "Font" tab, you can select a font and font size for the console window. You can also enable font smoothing and change the font type for bold and italic text.
- On the "Colors" tab, you can select the foreground and background colors for the console window. You can also customize the color scheme for various console elements, such as the text, background, popup, and cursor.
- Once you have configured the console settings, click on the "OK" button to save the changes.

You can also customize the PowerShell profile to configure the console environment. The profile is a script file that is executed when the PowerShell console starts. You can use the profile to define aliases, functions, variables, and modules that are loaded automatically.

To create or modify the PowerShell profile, open the PowerShell console and type "notepad $PROFILE". This will open the profile script file in Notepad. You can add your customizations to the profile script file, such as defining aliases and functions, setting environment variables, and importing modules. Save the changes to the file.

Once you have configured the console settings and profile, you can use the PowerShell console to manage and automate Windows environments. You can run commands, scripts, and modules to perform various administrative tasks, such as managing users and groups, configuring network settings, and monitoring system performance.

# Customize PowerShell Profile

The PowerShell profile is a useful feature that allows users to customize their PowerShell experience by running a script file each time the console is opened. This script file can be used to define aliases, functions, and variables that are specific to the user's needs, making it easier to access frequently used commands and automate common tasks. With a customized PowerShell profile, users can save time and increase their productivity by tailoring their console environment to their own unique needs and preferences. By leveraging the power of the PowerShell profile, users can take their console experience to the next level and streamline their workflow.

## Steps to Customize Profile

Following is the prcedure to customize the PowerShell profile:
- Open the PowerShell console by clicking on the Start menu and typing "PowerShell" in the search bar. Click on "Windows PowerShell" to open the console.
- Type "notepad $PROFILE" in the console and press Enter. This will open the profile script file in Notepad.
- If the profile script file doesn't exist, Notepad will prompt you to create it. Click "Yes" to create the file.

## Define Alias, Functions and Variables

In Notepad, you can define aliases, functions, and variables in the profile script file. Here are some examples:

Define an alias for a common command:

**Set-Alias ll Get-ChildItem -Force**

This will create an alias "ll" that runs the "Get-ChildItem -Force" command every time you type "ll" in the console.

Define a function to perform a specific task:

```
function Get-WebsiteStatus {
    $status = Invoke-WebRequest -Uri "https://www.example.com" -
UseBasicParsing
    if ($status.StatusCode -eq 200) {
        Write-Host "The website is up and running."
    } else {
        Write-Host "The website is down."
    }
}
```

This will create a function "Get-WebsiteStatus" that uses the "Invoke-WebRequest" cmdlet to check the status of a website. You can run this function by typing "Get-WebsiteStatus" in the console.

Define a variable to store a value:

```
$workspace = "C:\Users\UserName\Documents\Workspace"
```

This will create a variable "$workspace" that stores the path to a directory. You can use this variable in other commands and scripts. Once you have defined your aliases, functions, and variables, save the changes to the profile script file. Close and reopen the PowerShell console to see the changes take effect.

Now, every time you open the PowerShell console, your custom aliases, functions, and variables will be available to you. You can use them to simplify your work and increase your productivity.

# PowerShell ISE

## Overview

The PowerShell Integrated Scripting Environment (ISE) is an essential tool for system administrators and developers who work with PowerShell scripts and modules. It provides a graphical user interface (GUI) that simplifies the process of writing, testing, and debugging scripts. The ISE includes a rich text editor with syntax highlighting, code completion, and debugging tools, making it easier to create complex scripts without memorizing command-line syntax.

The ISE also features a script pane that displays the current script or module, a console pane that shows the output of commands and scripts, and a toolbar with buttons for common tasks like executing scripts and saving changes. Additionally, the ISE allows for multiple tabbed sessions, making it easy to work on multiple scripts or modules at the same time.

## PowerShell ISE Features

Following are some of the features of the PowerShell ISE:

- Intellisense: The ISE provides intelligent code completion, syntax highlighting, and parameter hinting to help you write PowerShell code faster and more accurately.
- Script debugging: The ISE includes a debugger that lets you step through your code line by line, set breakpoints, and inspect variables and objects in real-time.
- Multi-tab support: The ISE allows you to work on multiple scripts and modules simultaneously in separate tabs.
- Command history: The ISE maintains a command history that lets you recall and reuse previous commands and scripts.
- Script analyzer: The ISE includes a built-in script analyzer that checks your code for potential errors and provides suggestions for improving code quality.
- Output window: The ISE provides a console pane that displays the output of your commands and scripts.

The PowerShell ISE is included with Windows and can be accessed by clicking on the Start menu and typing "PowerShell ISE" in the search bar. It is a powerful tool for system administrators and developers who want to write and test PowerShell scripts in a user-friendly environment.

# PowerShell ISE vs. Visual Studio Code

PowerShell ISE (Integrated Scripting Environment) and Visual Studio Code (VS Code) are both popular tools for developing and testing PowerShell scripts. Here are some key differences between the two:

- User interface: PowerShell ISE has a more traditional user interface with a dedicated console pane and script editor, while VS Code is more modern with a customizable interface and a wider range of extensions.
- Debugging: PowerShell ISE has built-in debugging tools that allow you to step through code and inspect variables, while VS Code requires the installation of the PowerShell extension and a debugger to debug code.
- Code completion: PowerShell ISE provides IntelliSense for PowerShell commands and modules, while VS Code provides more comprehensive code completion and suggestions for other languages.

- Extensibility: VS Code is a more extensible tool, with a wide range of extensions for PowerShell and other languages, while PowerShell ISE has a limited set of features and is not as customizable.
- Platform support: VS Code is available on multiple platforms, including Windows, macOS, and Linux, while PowerShell ISE is only available on Windows.

Overall, PowerShell ISE is a good tool for basic PowerShell scripting and debugging, while Visual Studio Code is a more comprehensive tool with a wider range of features and customization options. However, if you are working exclusively on Windows and primarily using PowerShell, PowerShell ISE may be a better choice due to its ease of use and built-in tools. On the other hand, if you are working with multiple languages or platforms, VS Code may be a more versatile choice.

# PowerShell Syntax and Grammar

Let us take a look at some of the most commonly used PowerShell syntax and grammar along with simple examples:

## Variables

```
$variable = "Hello World"
Write-Output $variable
```

In the above given example, we create a variable called $variable and assign it the value "Hello World". We then use the Write-Output cmdlet to display the value of the variable.

## Strings

```
$string = "Hello World"
Write-Output $string
```

In the above given sample program, we create a string variable called $string and assign it the value "Hello World". We then use the Write-Output cmdlet to display the value of the string.

# Arrays

```
$array = "Item1", "Item2", "Item3"
Write-Output $array[1]
```

In the above given sample program, we create an array variable called $array and assign it three values. We then use the Write-Output cmdlet to display the second value in the array using the index [1].

# If Statements

```
$variable = "Hello"
if ($variable -eq "Hello") {
    Write-Output "The variable contains Hello"
} else {
    Write-Output "The variable does not contain Hello"
}
```

In the above given sample program, we create a variable called $variable and assign it the value "Hello". We then use an if statement to check if the value of the variable is "Hello". If it is, we display a message indicating that the variable contains "Hello". Otherwise, we display a message indicating that the variable does not contain "Hello".

# For Loops

```
for ($i = 0; $i -lt 5; $i++) {
    Write-Output "The value of i is: $i"
}
```

In the above given sample program, we use a for loop to iterate through the values of $i from 0 to 4. We then use the Write-Output cmdlet to display the value of $i in each iteration of the loop.

# While Loops

```
$i = 0
while ($i -lt 5) {
    Write-Output "The value of i is: $i"
    $i++
}
```

In the above given sample program, we use a while loop to iterate through the values of $i from 0 to 4. We then use the Write-Output cmdlet to display the value of $i in each iteration of the loop. We also increment the value of $i at the end of each iteration.

# Functions

```
function Add-Numbers {
    param($num1, $num2)
    $sum = $num1 + $num2
    Write-Output "The sum of $num1 and $num2 is: $sum"
}
```

```
Add-Numbers -num1 5 -num2 3
```

In the above given sample program, we create a function called Add-Numbers that takes two parameters $num1 and $num2. We then calculate the sum of the two parameters and display the result using the Write-Output cmdlet. We call the function and pass in the values 5 and 3 for $num1 and $num2.

The above ones are just a few examples of the many PowerShell syntax and grammar elements that you may encounter. It's important to practice and experiment with different PowerShell commands and scripts to become familiar with the language.

# CHAPTER 3: CMDLETS, ALIASES, AND FUNCTIONS

# Understanding Cmdlets

Cmdlets, also known as Commandlets, are essential components of PowerShell, a powerful automation and scripting tool developed by Microsoft. These small commands provide the fundamental building blocks for executing various tasks within a Windows environment. They are designed to be simple, efficient, and highly flexible, enabling system administrators and developers to automate complex administrative tasks with ease.

Cmdlets can be written in C# or PowerShell scripting language and follow a naming convention of Verb-Noun. The Verb-Noun naming convention reflects the command's action and the object being acted upon, making it easy to understand and use. For example, the "Get-Process" cmdlet retrieves information about running processes, and the "Stop-Service" cmdlet stops a running service.

One of the most significant advantages of using cmdlets is that they can easily integrate with other PowerShell commands through the pipeline, allowing output from one cmdlet to serve as input to another. This functionality enables system administrators to build complex automation workflows with ease, streamlining their day-to-day operations and reducing human error.

Cmdlets are also modular, which means they can be used selectively, reducing the overhead of loading large libraries of commands. With this modular approach, administrators can choose only the necessary cmdlets for a specific task, resulting in a more efficient use of resources.

# Popular 25 Cmdlets

Following are 25 popular cmdlets in PowerShell with sample commands:

- Get-Process: Retrieves information about running processes

Get-Process

- Get-Service: Retrieves information about Windows services

Get-Service

- Get-ChildItem: Retrieves information about files and directories

Get-ChildItem C:\Windows

Get-ItemProperty: Retrieves information about the properties of an item

Get-ItemProperty C:\Windows\System32\cmd.exe

- Set-Location: Changes the current location to a specified path

Set-Location C:\Windows\System32

- New-Item: Creates a new item in a specified location

New-Item C:\temp\newfile.txt

- Remove-Item: Deletes an item from a specified location

Remove-Item C:\temp\oldfile.txt

- Rename-Item: Renames an item at a specified location

Rename-Item C:\temp\file.txt newfile.txt

- Start-Process: Starts a new process

Start-Process notepad.exe

- Stop-Process: Stops a running process

Stop-Process -Name notepad

- Get-Content: Retrieves the contents of a file

Get-Content C:\temp\file.txt

- Set-Content: Sets the contents of a file to a specified value

Set-Content C:\temp\file.txt "Hello World"

- Out-File: Writes output to a file

Get-ChildItem | Out-File C:\temp\dirlist.txt

- Get-Date: Retrieves the current date and time

Get-Date

- Get-Host: Retrieves information about the local computer

Get-Host

- Get-Module: Retrieves information about loaded modules

Get-Module

- Import-Module: Loads a module into the current session

Import-Module ActiveDirectory

- Export-CSV: Exports output to a CSV file

Get-Process | Export-CSV C:\temp\processes.csv

- Test-Connection: Tests the connectivity to a remote host

Test-Connection google.com

- New-ADUser: Creates a new user account in Active Directory

```
New-ADUser -Name "John Doe" -GivenName "John" -Surname "Doe" -
UserPrincipalName "johndoe@contoso.com" -AccountPassword (ConvertTo-
SecureString "P@ssw0rd1" -AsPlainText -Force)
```

- Get-ADUser: Retrieves information about a user account in Active Directory

```
Get-ADUser -Identity johndoe
```

- Set-ADUser: Modifies a user account in Active Directory

```
Set-ADUser -Identity johndoe -Department "IT"
```

- Get-ADComputer: Retrieves information about a computer account in Active Directory

```
Get-ADComputer -Identity computer1
```

- Enable-ADAccount: Enables a disabled user or computer account in Active Directory

```
Enable-ADAccount -Identity johndoe
```

- Disable-ADAccount: Disables an enabled user or computer account in Active Directory

```
Disable-ADAccount -Identity johndoe
```

PowerShell offers a vast library of cmdlets that enable system administrators to automate and simplify numerous administrative tasks. Whether it's managing file systems, manipulating data, configuring network settings, or performing system maintenance, cmdlets provide a powerful toolset for achieving these tasks. By learning and mastering the use of cmdlets, system administrators can streamline their workflows, reduce errors, and boost productivity. This can lead to better resource utilization, improved system performance, and greater efficiency in managing complex IT environments.

# PowerShell Aliases

In PowerShell, aliases are alternative names for cmdlets, functions, and scripts. Aliases are used to simplify the syntax of commands, making them easier to remember and type. Aliases are important for system administrators because they allow them to work more efficiently and effectively by reducing the amount of typing required to execute common tasks. Aliases also allow administrators to customize their PowerShell environment, making it easier to work with and more tailored to their specific needs.

## Create Alias

To create an alias, use the Set-Alias cmdlet with the desired name and cmdlet:

Set-Alias -Name ls -Value Get-ChildItem

In the above given sample program, we create an alias called ls that runs the Get-ChildItem cmdlet.

## Modify Alias

To modify an existing alias, use the Set-Alias cmdlet with the new cmdlet:

Set-Alias -Name ls -Value Get-Item

In the above given sample program, we modify the ls alias to run the Get-Item cmdlet instead of Get-ChildItem.

## Remove Alias

To remove an alias, use the Remove-Item cmdlet with the alias name:

Remove-Item alias:ls

In the above given sample program, we remove the ls alias from our PowerShell environment.

There are two types of aliases in PowerShell: built-in aliases and custom aliases. Built-in aliases are pre-defined aliases that are provided by PowerShell, while custom aliases are aliases that you create yourself.

## Custom Alias

Creating a custom alias:

Set-Alias -Name show -Value Get-Service

In the above given sample program, we create a custom alias called show that runs the Get-Service cmdlet.

## Modify Existing Alias

Modifying an existing alias:

Set-Alias -Name cls -Value Clear-Host

In the above given sample program, we modify the built-in cls alias to run the Clear-Host cmdlet instead of Clear-Content.

## Remove Custom Alias

Removing a custom alias:

Remove-Item alias:show

In the above given sample program, we remove the show alias from our PowerShell environment. By using aliases effectively, system administrators can simplify their work and improve their productivity in PowerShell. It's important to keep in mind that aliases should be used sparingly and only when they make commands easier to remember and type.

# PowerShell Functions

PowerShell functions are powerful tools that enable users to create custom commands to perform specific tasks in a more efficient manner. By breaking down complex tasks into smaller, more manageable chunks of code, PowerShell functions can make writing and maintaining scripts much easier. They also make it easier to reuse code and share functions with others, which can be especially helpful in a team environment. Functions in PowerShell allow users to pass input parameters and perform actions based on that input, making them highly customizable and versatile. Whether you are a beginner or an experienced user, understanding how to create and use PowerShell functions can greatly enhance your productivity and efficiency.

# Naming Functions

In PowerShell, function names should follow the same conventions as cmdlets, using the Verb-Noun naming pattern. The verb should describe the action performed by the function, and the noun should describe the object being acted upon. For example, a function that retrieves information about running processes might be called Get-ProcessInfo.

# Declaring Functions

To declare a function in PowerShell, use the function keyword followed by the name of the function and any parameters. The code block for the function is enclosed in curly braces {}.

Following is an example of a simple function that takes two parameters and adds them together:

```
function Add-Numbers {
    param($num1, $num2)
    $sum = $num1 + $num2
    Write-Output "The sum of $num1 and $num2 is: $sum"
}
```

# Parameters

Functions in PowerShell can accept parameters, which allow you to pass values to the function and customize its behavior. Parameters are declared using the param keyword followed by the parameter name. You can also specify default values for parameters by assigning a value after the parameter name.

Following is an example of a function that accepts a parameter with a default value:

```
function Get-ProcessInfo {
    param($name = "notepad")
    Get-Process $name
}
```

In the above example, we declare a function called Get-ProcessInfo that accepts a parameter called $name. If no value is provided for $name, the function defaults to using "notepad". The function then runs the Get-Process cmdlet using the value of $name.

# Popular Common Functions

The given below are the most popular and commonly in-use functions of PowerShell:

- Get-ChildItem: Retrieves information about files and directories.
- Get-Process: Retrieves information about running processes.
- Get-Service: Retrieves information about Windows services.
- Get-ItemProperty: Retrieves information about the properties of an item.
- Set-Location: Changes the current location to a specified path.
- New-Item: Creates a new item in a specified location.
- Remove-Item: Deletes an item from a specified location.
- Rename-Item: Renames an item at a specified location.
- Start-Process: Starts a new process.
- Stop-Process: Stops a running process.

# Advanced Functions

Advanced functions in PowerShell are designed to perform complex tasks and provide enhanced features such as the ability to handle errors gracefully, accept input from the pipeline, and validate parameters. These functions are ideal for automating repetitive tasks, improving efficiency, and increasing productivity.

Following are the ten advanced functions in PowerShell with examples of how to declare them:

*Function with pipeline support*

```php
Copy code
function Get-Users {
    [CmdletBinding()]
    param(
        [Parameter(ValueFromPipeline=$true)]
        [string[]]$usernames
    )
```

```
process {
    foreach ($username in $usernames) {
        Get-ADUser -Identity $username
    }
  }
}
```

In the above given sample program, we declare a function called Get-Users that accepts input from the pipeline. The function uses the process block to iterate through the input and run the Get-ADUser cmdlet for each input value.

## Function with parameter validation

```
function Set-ServiceStatus {
    [CmdletBinding()]
    param(
        [Parameter(Mandatory=$true)]
        [string]$service,
        [ValidateSet("Running", "Stopped")]
        [string]$status
)
Set-Service -Name $service -Status $status
}
```

In the above given sample program, we declare a function called `Set-ServiceStatus` that sets the status of a specified service. The function uses the `[ValidateSet()]` attribute to restrict the valid values for the `$status` parameter to "Running" and "Stopped".

## Function with error handling

```
function Get-ProcessInfo {
[CmdletBinding()]
param(
[Parameter(Mandatory=$true)]
```

```
[string]$name
)
try {
Get-Process $name -ErrorAction Stop
}
catch {
Write-Warning "Process not found"
}
}
```

In the above given sample program, we declare a function called `Get-ProcessInfo` that retrieves information about a specified process. The function uses a `try`/`catch` block to handle errors that might occur when running the `Get-Process` cmdlet. If the cmdlet fails, the catch block writes a warning message.

*Function with default parameter values*

```
function Get-ChildItemDetails {
[CmdletBinding()]
param(
[string]$path = $PWD.Path,
[switch]$recurse
)
if ($recurse) {
Get-ChildItem $path -Recurse | Format-List
}
else {
Get-ChildItem $path | Format-List
}
}
```

In the above given sample program, we declare a function called `Get-ChildItemDetails` that retrieves detailed information about files and directories in a specified location. The function uses a default value of the current working directory for the `$path` parameter and a switch parameter called `$recurse` that controls whether to recursively search subdirectories.

## Function with multiple output streams

```
function Get-ProcessInfo {
[CmdletBinding()]
param(
[Parameter(Mandatory=$true)]
[string]$name
)
$process = Get-Process $name -ErrorAction SilentlyContinue
if ($process) {
Write-Output $process
}
else {
Write-Error "Process not found"
}
}
```

In the above given sample program, we declare a function called `Get-ProcessInfo` that retrieves information about a specified process. The function uses a conditional statement to check if the process was found and then writes the output to the pipeline. If the process was not found, the function writes an error message to the error stream.

## Function with multiple parameter sets

```
function Get-File {
[CmdletBinding(DefaultParameterSetName="Path")]
param(
[Parameter(Mandatory=$true, ParameterSetName="Path")]
[string]$path,
[Parameter(Mandatory=$true, ParameterSetName="ID")]
[int]$id
```

```
)
if ($id) {
Get-FileById $id
}
else {
Get-FileByPath $path
}
}
```

In the above given sample program, we declare a function called `Get-File` that retrieves a file by either its path or ID. The function uses multiple parameter sets to allow users to specify either a path or ID as input.

*Function with dynamic parameters*

```
function Get-ADObject {
[CmdletBinding()]
param(
[Parameter(Mandatory=$true)]
[string]$type
)
DynamicParam {
$properties = Get-ADObjectPropertyList $type
$paramDictionary = New-Object -Type PSObject
foreach ($property in $properties) {
$attribute = New-Object -Type
System.Management.Automation.RuntimeDefinedParameter($property,
[string], $null)
$attributeDictionary = New-Object -Type
System.Management.Automation.RuntimeDefinedParameterDictionary
    $attributeDictionary.Add($property, $attribute)
    $paramDictionary.PSObject.Properties.Add($attribute)
}
```

```
    return $paramDictionary
}
process {
    $properties = $PSBoundParameters.Keys
    Get-ADObjectProperties -Type $type -Properties $properties
}
}
```

In the above given sample program, we declare a function called `Get-ADObject` that retrieves information about an Active Directory object of a specified type. The function uses dynamic parameters to create input parameters based on the object's properties.

*Function with output formatting*

```
function Get-ServiceInfo {
[CmdletBinding()]
param(
[Parameter(Mandatory=$true)]
[string]$name
)
$service = Get-Service $name -ErrorAction SilentlyContinue
if ($service) {
$service | Select-Object -Property Name, Status, DisplayName | Format-Table -
AutoSize
}
else {
Write-Error "Service not found"
}
}
```

In the above given sample program, we declare a function called `Get-ServiceInfo` that retrieves information about a specified Windows service. The function uses the `Select-Object` cmdlet to select the properties to display and the `Format-Table` cmdlet to format the output as a table.

## Function with pipeline input

```
function Get-ProcessInfo {
[CmdletBinding()]
param(
[Parameter(ValueFromPipeline=$true)]
[string[]]$names
)
process {
foreach ($name in $names) {
Get-Process $name
}
}
}
```

In the above given sample program, we declare a function called `Get-ProcessInfo` that retrieves information about running processes. The function accepts input from the pipeline and uses the `process` block to iterate through the input and run the `Get-Process` cmdlet for each input value.

## Function with output to file

```
function Export-CSV {
[CmdletBinding()]
param(
[Parameter(Mandatory=$true)]
[string]$path
)
$items = Get-ChildItem
$items | Export-Csv $path -NoTypeInformation
}
```

In the above given sample program, we declare a function called `Export-CSV` that exports information about files and directories to a CSV file. The function uses the `Get-ChildItem` cmdlet to retrieve the information and the `Export-Csv` cmdlet to write the information to a file.

By learning how to create and use functions in PowerShell, system administrators can write efficient and reusable code to automate complex tasks. With advanced functions, they can add error handling, input validation, and other advanced features to make their code more robust and reliable.

# CHAPTER 4: UP AND RUNNING WITH SCRIPTING BASICS

PowerShell is a powerful scripting language and automation framework that is widely used in the Microsoft ecosystem. It is designed to help system administrators automate tasks and manage systems efficiently. PowerShell relies heavily on variables to store and manipulate data, which are defined using a dollar sign prefix. The language supports various data types, including strings, integers, and arrays. PowerShell also provides a wide range of operators, such as arithmetic, comparison, and logical operators, to perform operations on variables and data types.

# Variables

PowerShell is a popular command-line interface used to automate tasks in Windows environments. One of its key features is the ability to use variables to store and manipulate data. A variable is simply a named storage location that can hold a value, such as a string, integer, or object. PowerShell variables are case-insensitive and can be assigned values using the "$" symbol followed by the variable name. Variables can also be used to reference other variables or command output, making them a powerful tool for scripting and automation. By using variables, PowerShell users can streamline their workflow, automate repetitive tasks, and create more efficient and effective scripts.

## Creating and using variables

To create a variable in PowerShell, you use the dollar sign ($) followed by the variable name. You can assign a value to a variable using the assignment operator (=). Given below is an example:

```
$name = "John Doe"
$age = 30
```

In the above given example, we created two variables: $name and $age. The $name variable stores a string value ("John Doe"), while the $age variable stores an integer value (30).

To access the value stored in a variable, you simply reference the variable by its name. For example:

```
Write-Host "Name: $name"
Write-Host "Age: $age"
```

This will output:

Name: John Doe
Age: 30

# Variable scope

PowerShell employs various variable scopes to manage the visibility and accessibility of variables. These scopes include global, local, script, and private, each of which defines a specific area where a variable can be accessed and modified. A global variable can be accessed throughout the script, while a local variable is limited to a specific function or script block. A script variable is accessible within the script in which it is defined, while a private variable can only be accessed within the scope in which it is declared. Understanding variable scopes is crucial for effective PowerShell scripting.

## Global

A global variable can be accessed from any part of the script and any scripts that the current script runs. To declare a global variable, you use the $global: prefix before the variable name:

$global:myGlobalVar = "This is a global variable"

## Local

A local variable is accessible only within the current scope, such as a function or script block. To declare a local variable, you can simply use the $ prefix before the variable name, or you can use the $local: prefix to be more explicit:

$local:myLocalVar = "This is a local variable"

## Script

A script variable is accessible within the script file where it is defined and any child scopes, such as functions or script blocks within the script. To declare a script variable, you use the $script: prefix before the variable name:

$script:myScriptVar = "This is a script variable"

## Private

A private variable is accessible only within the current scope and cannot be accessed from child scopes. To declare a private variable, you use the $private: prefix before the variable name:

```
$private:myPrivateVar = "This is a private variable"
```

# Data Types

PowerShell has access to the rich set of data types and functions provided by .NET. This enables PowerShell to handle a wide range of data types, including strings, integers, arrays, and more, making it a versatile tool for automation and administration tasks. Here are some of the most common data types used in PowerShell:

## String

A string is a sequence of characters, typically used to represent text. You can create a string in PowerShell by enclosing a sequence of characters in single or double quotes:

```
$singleQuoteString = 'This is a string using single quotes'
$doubleQuoteString = "This is a string using double quotes"
```

## Integer

An integer is a whole number without a fractional component. In PowerShell, integers can be signed (positive or negative) or unsigned (positive only). Here are some examples:

```
$signedInt = -42
$unsignedInt = 42
```

## Float and Double

Float and double are both used to represent floating-point numbers, which are numbers with a decimal point. Float is a single-precision floating-point number, while double is a double-precision floating-point number. The difference between them lies in the number of bits used to store the value and the precision they can represent.

```
$floatNumber = 3.14f
$doubleNumber = 3.14
```

# Boolean

A boolean data type represents true or false values. In PowerShell, boolean values are represented by the $true and $false keywords:

```
$isValid = $true
$isReady = $false
```

# Array

An array is a collection of elements, where each element can be of any data type. In PowerShell, you can create an array using the @() syntax:

```
$myArray = @(1, 2, 3, 4, 5)
```

You can also create an array by simply separating values with commas:

```
$myArray = 1, 2, 3, 4, 5
```

# Hashtable

A hashtable is a collection of key-value pairs, where each key is associated with a value. In PowerShell, you can create a hashtable using the @{} syntax:

```
$myHashtable = @{
    Key1 = 'Value1'
    Key2 = 'Value2'
    Key3 = 'Value3'
}
```

# Operators

Operators in PowerShell are used to perform operations on values and variables. There are various types of operators in PowerShell, such as arithmetic, comparison, assignment, and logical operators.

## Arithmetic operators

Arithmetic operators are used to perform mathematical operations, such as addition, subtraction, multiplication, and division. Here are some examples:

```
$sum = 10 + 20        # 30
$difference = 30 - 10   # 20
$product = 10 * 20      # 200
$quotient = 30 / 10     # 3
$remainder = 30 % 7     # 2
```

## Comparison operators

Comparison operators are used to compare two values and return a boolean result ($true or $false). Some common comparison operators are:

- -eq: Equal to
- -ne: Not equal to
- -gt: Greater than
- -ge: Greater than or equal to
- -lt: Less than
- -le: Less than or equal to

Here are some examples:

```
$isEqual = 10 -eq 20    # False
$isNotEqual = 10 -ne 20 # True
$isGreater = 10 -gt 20  # False
```

## Assignment operators

Assignment operators are used to assign a value to a variable. The most basic assignment operator is =, which assigns a value to a variable:

```
$number = 42
```

PowerShell also supports compound assignment operators that perform an operation and

assignment in a single step. Here are some examples:
- +=: Add and assign
- -=: Subtract and assign
- *=: Multiply and assign
- /=: Divide and assign
- %=: Modulus and assign

```
$number = 10
$number += 5  # $number = $number + 5, now $number is 15
$number -= 3  # $number = $number - 3, now $number is 12
$number *= 2  # $number = $number * 2, now $number is 24
```

### Logical operators

Logical operators are used to perform operations on boolean values, such as AND, OR, and NOT. Some common logical operators in PowerShell are:
- -and: Logical AND
- -or: Logical OR
- -not: Logical NOT
- !: Logical NOT (alternative syntax)

Here are some examples:

```
$isTrue = $true -and $false  # False
$isFalse = $true -or $false  # True
$isNotTrue = -not $true      # False
$isNotFalse = !$false        # True
```

By understanding these fundamental concepts, you will be better equipped to write efficient and powerful PowerShell scripts. As you continue to explore PowerShell, you will discover even more advanced features and techniques

# Conditional Statements and Loops

PowerShell provides conditional statements such as "if/else" and "switch" to execute different actions based on specific conditions. Additionally, PowerShell offers various loop constructs such as "for" and "while" to perform repetitive tasks. These constructs are essential for effective PowerShell scripting and allow for greater control and automation of tasks. In this section, we'll discuss the commonly used conditional statements and loops in PowerShell.

# Conditional Statements

Conditional statements are used to perform different actions based on whether a specified condition is true or false. PowerShell supports two main conditional statements: if and switch.

## *If Statement*

The if statement is used to test a condition and execute a block of code if the condition is true. You can also use the optional elseif and else clauses to test additional conditions or provide a default block of code if none of the conditions are true.

Given below is the syntax for an if statement in PowerShell:

```
if (condition) {
    # Code to execute if the condition is true
} elseif (another_condition) {
    # Code to execute if the another_condition is true
} else {
    # Code to execute if none of the conditions are true
}
```

For example:

```
$age = 18

if ($age -lt 18) {
    Write-Host "You are a minor."
} elseif ($age -eq 18) {
    Write-Host "You just turned adult."
} else {
    Write-Host "You are an adult."
}
```

## Switch Statement

The switch statement is used to select one of many code blocks to be executed based on the value of a specified variable or expression. It's especially useful when you have multiple conditions to test on a single value.

Given below is the syntax for a switch statement in PowerShell:

```
switch (value) {
   case_value1 {
    # Code to execute if value matches case_value1
}
case_value2 {
   # Code to execute if value matches case_value2
}
default {
   # Code to execute if none of the case values match
}
}
```

For example:

```
$dayOfWeek = "Tuesday"

switch ($dayOfWeek) {
   "Monday" {
      Write-Host "Today is Monday."
   }
   "Tuesday" {
      Write-Host "Today is Tuesday."
   }
   "Wednesday" {
      Write-Host "Today is Wednesday."
   }
```

```
default {
    Write-Host "Not a valid day."
  }
}
```

# Loops

Loops are used to execute a block of code repeatedly until a specified condition is met. PowerShell supports several types of loops, including for, foreach, while, and do-while.

## For Loop

The for loop is used to execute a block of code a specific number of times. It consists of three parts: initialization, condition, and increment/decrement.

Given below is the syntax for a for loop in PowerShell:

```
for (initialization; condition; increment/decrement) {
    # Code to execute repeatedly
}
```

For example:

```
for ($i = 1; $i -le 5; $i++) {
    Write-Host "Iteration: $i"
}
```

## Foreach Loop

The foreach loop is used to iterate through a collection of items, such as an array or a list. It executes a block of code for each item in the collection.

Given below is the syntax for a foreach loop in PowerShell:

```
foreach ($item in collection) {
# Code to execute for each item
}
```

For example:

```
$names = @("Alice", "Bob", "Carol", "David")

foreach ($name in $names) {
    Write-Host "Hello, $name!"
}
```

## While Loop

The while loop is used to execute a block of code as long as a specified condition is true. If the condition is false when the loop is first encountered, the code block will not be executed at all.

Given below is the syntax for a while loop in PowerShell:

```
while (condition) {
    # Code to execute repeatedly while the condition is true
}
```

For example:

```
$counter = 1

while ($counter -le 5) {
    Write-Host "Counter: $counter"
    $counter++
}
```

## Do-While Loop

The do-while loop is similar to the while loop, but it checks the condition at the end of the loop instead of the beginning. This means that the code block will always be executed at least once, even if the condition is false.

Given below is the syntax for a do-while loop in PowerShell:

```
do {
    # Code to execute repeatedly while the condition is true
} while (condition)
```

For example:

```
$counter = 1

do {
    Write-Host "Counter: $counter"
    $counter++
} while ($counter -le 5)
```

Conditional statements and loops are fundamental constructs in PowerShell that allow you to control the flow of your script and perform repetitive tasks efficiently. By understanding how to use if, switch, for, foreach, while, and do-while, you will be able to write more flexible and powerful PowerShell scripts.

# Best Practices

Here are a few additional tips to help you get the most out of loops and conditional statements in PowerShell:

- When working with large collections or complex conditions, be mindful of performance. Optimize your loops and conditions to minimize the time it takes to execute your script.

- Use descriptive variable names and proper indentation to make your loops and conditional statements more readable and easier to maintain.

- Consider using functions and modules to break down complex loops and conditional statements into smaller, more manageable pieces.

- Test your loops and conditional statements thoroughly to ensure they behave as expected, especially when dealing with edge cases and unusual input values.

# PowerShell Pipeline

The PowerShell pipeline is a powerful feature that allows you to pass the output of one command (or cmdlet) directly as input to another command. This enables you to chain multiple commands together, allowing you to perform complex operations on data with ease.

The pipeline is represented by the pipe character (|) and is used to separate commands in a pipeline.

Given below is a simple example of using the pipeline:

```
Get-Process | Where-Object { $_.CPU -gt 100 } | Format-Table -AutoSize
```

In the above given example, we're using the Get-Process cmdlet to retrieve the list of running processes, then filtering the list to only include processes with a CPU usage greater than 100 using the Where-Object cmdlet, and finally formatting the output as an auto-sized table using the Format-Table cmdlet.

## Common Pipeline Cmdlets

Here are some commonly used cmdlets in the PowerShell pipeline:
- Where-Object: Filters input objects based on a specified condition.
- ForEach-Object: Executes a script block for each input object.
- Sort-Object: Sorts input objects based on specified properties.
- Select-Object: Selects specific properties from input objects or creates new objects with the specified properties.
- Group-Object: Groups input objects based on specified properties.
- Measure-Object: Calculates the numeric properties of input objects, such as the count, sum, or average.
- Export-Csv: Exports input objects to a CSV file.

Given below is a more complex example that demonstrates the use of multiple pipeline cmdlets:

```
Get-ChildItem -Path "C:\Users" -Recurse -File |
Where-Object { $_.Extension -eq ".txt" } |
ForEach-Object { Add-Content -Path $_.FullName -Value "`n-EOF-" } |
Select-Object FullName, Length |
```

```
Sort-Object Length -Descending |
Export-Csv -Path "ModifiedFiles.csv" -NoTypeInformation
```

In the above given sample program, we're using the Get-ChildItem cmdlet to retrieve all text files in the "C:\Users" directory and its subdirectories, appending "-EOF-" to the end of each file using ForEach-Object, selecting the FullName and Length properties, sorting the files by their Length property in descending order, and finally exporting the results to a CSV file.

# Output Formatting

PowerShell provides several cmdlets to help you format the output of your scripts and commands. These cmdlets allow you to control the appearance of the output, making it more readable and easier to understand.

## Format-Table

The Format-Table cmdlet displays the output in a table format, with each property of the input objects represented as a column. You can use the -AutoSize switch to automatically adjust the column widths based on the content.

Example:

```
Get-Process | Format-Table -Property Name, CPU, Memory -AutoSize
```

## Format-List

The Format-List cmdlet displays the output in a list format, with each property of the input objects represented as a separate line. This is useful when you have objects with many properties or when the properties have long values.

Example:

```
Get-Service | Where-Object { $_.Status -eq "Running" } | Format-List -Property Name, DisplayName, Status
```

## Format-Wide

The Format-Wide cmdlet displays the output in a wide format, with each property of the input objects represented as a single column that spans the entire width of the console. This is useful when you only need to display a single property for each object.

Example:

Get-ChildItem | Format-Wide -Property Name -Column 3

# Format-Custom

The Format-Custom cmdlet allows you to create a custom view of the output by specifying a script block that defines the layout and appearance of the properties. This is useful when you need to create a highly customized output format.

Example:

```
Get-Process | Format-Custom -Property Name, CPU, Memory -Expression {
    "Process: " + $_.Name
    "CPU: " + $_.CPU
    "Memory: " + $_.Memory
    "-----"
}
```

PowerShell's pipeline and output formatting features are crucial for efficiently processing and manipulating data. By understanding how to use the pipeline and format the output, you can create powerful and flexible scripts that perform complex operations.

# CHAPTER 5: WORKING WITH POWERSHELL MODULES

# Introduction to Modules

In PowerShell, modules are packages that contain reusable code, including cmdlets, functions, scripts, and other resources. They help you manage and organize your PowerShell environment, allowing you to import, export, and share functionality across different scripts and sessions.

Here are some key aspects of PowerShell modules:

Structure: A PowerShell module is a collection of files, typically containing a .psm1 (script module) file, a .psd1 (module manifest) file, and optionally, a .ps1xml (formatting and type data) file. The module manifest (.psd1) contains metadata about the module, such as the author, version, and dependencies, while the .psm1 file holds the actual code and functions.

Importing and Exporting: To make a module available for use, you need to import it into your PowerShell session using the Import-Module cmdlet, followed by the module name or path. Once imported, you can access and use the cmdlets, functions, and other resources from that module. To remove a module from your session, use the Remove-Module cmdlet.

Built-in Modules: PowerShell comes with several built-in modules, such as the Microsoft.PowerShell.Management and Microsoft.PowerShell.Utility modules. You can use these modules to perform various tasks, such as managing files, processes, and services.

Custom Modules: You can create your own custom modules by writing PowerShell code and saving it as a .psm1 file. This allows you to create reusable functionality that can be shared across different scripts and sessions.

To create a custom module, follow these steps:
- Write your functions and code in a PowerShell script file and save it with a .psm1 extension, for example, MyModule.psm1.
- Create a module manifest using the New-ModuleManifest cmdlet. This cmdlet generates a .psd1 file that contains metadata about your module, such as author, version, dependencies, and exported commands.
- Save your module in one of the directories specified in the $env:PSModulePath environment variable, which are the default locations where PowerShell looks for modules. Alternatively, you can save it in a custom directory and provide the full path when importing the module.

Discovering Modules: To find available modules on your system, use the Get-Module cmdlet with the -ListAvailable parameter. This cmdlet returns a list of all modules that are installed and available for import.

Installing Modules: You can install additional modules from the PowerShell Gallery, which is an online repository for PowerShell modules and scripts, using the Install-Module cmdlet. For example, to install a module named "ExampleModule", you would run: Install-Module -Name ExampleModule.

Updating Modules: To update an installed module, use the Update-Module cmdlet. This cmdlet checks the PowerShell Gallery for a newer version of the specified module and updates it if available.

Remember that when working with modules in a production environment, it's a best practice to test them in a controlled environment first to ensure compatibility and functionality.

# Importing and Exporting Modules

Importing and exporting modules in PowerShell is done using the Import-Module and Export-ModuleMember cmdlets. Given below is a step-by-step guide on how to import and export modules with a sample program.

## Create Custom PowerShell Module

First, create a custom PowerShell module with a simple function. Open a text editor and add the following code:

```
function Get-Greeting {
    param (
        [string]$Name = "User"
    )
    "Hello, $Name!"
}
```

Save this file as MyGreetingModule.psm1 in a directory of your choice.

## Import Custom Module

To import the module into your PowerShell session, you can use the Import-Module cmdlet followed by the module path:

```
Import-Module -Name "C:\path\to\MyGreetingModule.psm1"
```

Replace "C:\path\to" with the actual directory where you saved the MyGreetingModule.psm1 file.

## Use Function from Imported Module

Now that the module is imported, you can use the Get-Greeting function in your session:

```
Get-Greeting -Name "John"
```

This should output:

Hello, John!

## Export Specific Functions from Module

If you want to export only specific functions from the module, you can use the Export-ModuleMember cmdlet inside the module. Add the following line to your MyGreetingModule.psm1 file after the function definition:

```
Export-ModuleMember -Function Get-Greeting
```

This line exports only the Get-Greeting function from the module.

## Import Specific Functions

To import only the exported functions, use the Import-Module cmdlet with the -Function parameter:

```
Import-Module -Name "C:\path\to\MyGreetingModule.psm1" -Function Get-Greeting
```

This imports only the Get-Greeting function from the module.

Given below is the complete code example:

```
# MyGreetingModule.psm1
function Get-Greeting {
  param (
    [string]$Name = "User"
  )
  "Hello, $Name!"
}

Export-ModuleMember -Function Get-Greeting

# Import the module
Import-Module -Name "C:\path\to\MyGreetingModule.psm1" -Function Get-Greeting

# Use the function
Get-Greeting -Name "John"
```

This should output:

Hello, John!

In the above given sample program, we created a custom module with a single function, imported it into our PowerShell session, and used the function from the module. We also demonstrated how to export only specific functions from the module and how to import them into our session.

# Creating Custom Modules

Following below is a step-by-step guide on how to create a custom module and modify it using a sample program:

## Create a PowerShell Script

First, create a new PowerShell script file with some functions that you want to include in your module. For example, let us create a script called MyModuleFunctions.ps1 with the following code:

```
function Get-MyModuleVersion {
    "1.0"
}


function Get-MyModuleAuthor {
    "Your Name"
}


function Get-MyModuleDescription {
    "This is a sample module."
}
```

Save the MyModuleFunctions.ps1 file in a directory of your choice.

## Create Module Manifest File

Next, you need to create a module manifest file that describes the module and its contents. Open a text editor and create a new file called MyModule.psd1. Add the following lines to the file:

```
@{
    ModuleVersion = '1.0'
    Author = 'Your Name'
    Description = 'This is a sample module.'
    FunctionsToExport = 'Get-MyModuleVersion', 'Get-MyModuleAuthor', 'Get-MyModuleDescription'
}
```

This manifest specifies the module version, author, description, and the functions to export from the module.

Save the MyModule.psd1 file in the same directory as the MyModuleFunctions.ps1 file.

# Create the Module File

Now that you have the script file and module manifest, you can create the module file itself. Open a new file in your text editor and add the following lines:

```
# Import the functions from the script file
. $PSScriptRoot\MyModuleFunctions.ps1

# Export the functions specified in the manifest
Export-ModuleMember -Function Get-MyModuleVersion, Get-MyModuleAuthor, Get-MyModuleDescription
```

This code imports the functions from the MyModuleFunctions.ps1 script file and exports the functions specified in the MyModule.psd1 manifest.

Save this file with the name MyModule.psm1 in the same directory as the other files.

# Test the Module

To test the module, open a new PowerShell session and navigate to the directory where you saved the MyModule.psm1 file. Then, import the module using the Import-Module cmdlet:

```
Import-Module .\MyModule.psm1
```

Now, you can use the functions in the module:

```
PS> Get-MyModuleVersion
1.0

PS> Get-MyModuleAuthor
Your Name

PS> Get-MyModuleDescription
```

This is a sample module.

# Modify the Module

To modify the module, open the MyModuleFunctions.ps1 file in your text editor and add a new function:

```
function Get-MyModuleName {
  "MyModule"
}
```

Save the file.

Now, open the MyModule.psm1 file in your text editor and modify it to include the new function:

```
# Import the functions from the script file
. $PSScriptRoot\MyModuleFunctions.ps1

# Export the functions specified in the manifest
Export-ModuleMember -Function Get-MyModuleVersion, Get-MyModuleAuthor, Get-MyModuleDescription, Get-MyModuleName
```

Save the file.

# Test the Modified Module

To test the modified module, import it again in your PowerShell session:

```
Import-Module .\MyModule.psm1
```

Now, you can use the new function in the module:

```
PS> Get-MyModuleName
MyModule
```

This demonstrates how to modify an existing custom module by adding a new function to the script file, then importing and exporting it in the MyModule.psm1 file. Once the module is imported again, the new function is available for use.

In summary, creating a custom PowerShell module involves writing PowerShell functions in a script file, creating a module manifest file to describe the module and its contents, and creating a module file that imports the functions and exports them as specified in the manifest. Once the module is created, it can be imported into a PowerShell session and used like any other PowerShell module. Modifying an existing module involves updating the script file, then updating the module file to import and export the new functions.

# Popular Built-in and Community Modules

The given below are some popular built-in and community modules used by expert PowerShell users:

## Built-in Modules

Microsoft.PowerShell.Management - provides cmdlets for managing Windows processes, services, event logs, and more.

Microsoft.PowerShell.Utility - provides general-purpose cmdlets, such as ConvertTo-Json, Out-File, Get-Random, and more.

ActiveDirectory - provides cmdlets for managing Active Directory objects, such as users, groups, and computers.

NetSecurity - provides cmdlets for managing network security, such as firewalls, security groups, and network policies.

## Community Modules

PSWindowsUpdate - provides cmdlets for managing Windows updates, including searching for updates, downloading and installing updates, and managing update settings.

Pester - provides a testing framework for PowerShell, allowing users to write and run tests against PowerShell functions and scripts.

PowerCLI - provides cmdlets for managing VMware vSphere environments, allowing users to automate tasks and manage virtual machines and hosts.

PSReadline - provides enhanced command-line editing and history capabilities for PowerShell, including syntax highlighting, tab completion, and more.

These are just a few examples of popular built-in and community modules used by expert PowerShell users. There are many more modules available for specific use cases, such as managing Azure resources, automating Office 365 tasks, and working with JSON and REST APIs.

# CHAPTER 6: POWERSHELL SCRIPTING

PowerShell scripts are collections of commands that are executed in a sequential manner to achieve specific tasks. In this response, we will discuss writing, editing, and executing PowerShell scripts. PowerShell scripts are written using a text editor, such as Notepad or Visual Studio Code. Scripts are saved with the ".ps1" extension, and can be created from scratch or by copying and modifying existing scripts. PowerShell scripts consist of commands, which are executed in sequence, and can include loops, conditionals, functions, and variables. PowerShell has a vast library of built-in cmdlets that can be used in scripts, and there are many third-party modules available as well.

PowerShell scripts can be edited using any text editor, but it's recommended to use an editor with syntax highlighting and code completion features. Visual Studio Code is a popular choice for editing PowerShell scripts as it provides an integrated development environment (IDE) experience with features such as debugging and Git integration. PowerShell ISE (Integrated Scripting Environment) is another tool that provides a GUI for editing and debugging PowerShell scripts.

# Writing and Executing Scripts

## Plan your Script

Planning your script is an essential step in writing error-free PowerShell scripts. Before you start writing your script, take the time to consider what it should do. This will help you identify the cmdlets, variables, and functions that you need to include in your script.

One way to plan your script is to write down the steps it needs to take to accomplish its goal. This will help you visualize the script's structure and make it easier to write. For example, if you are writing a script to create a new user account in Active Directory, your steps might look something like this:
- Prompt the user for input (e.g., username, password, email address, etc.)
- Check if the user account already exists
- If the account does not exist, create a new user account
- Set the user's properties (e.g., password, email address, etc.)

By planning your script in this way, you can ensure that it is focused on accomplishing its intended purpose.

## Use Meaningful Variable Names

When defining variables in your script, use meaningful names that describe the data they represent. This makes your code more readable and easier to understand. For example, instead of using a variable name like "$x", use a name like "$username" to represent a user's username.

Using meaningful variable names helps you avoid confusion and reduces the likelihood of errors in your script. It also makes your code more accessible to others who may need to read or modify it in the future.

# Test your Script

Testing your script is an important step in ensuring that it is error-free. Before running your script in a production environment, test it on a small set of data or test environment. This helps you identify any errors or issues that need to be resolved before running the script in a production environment.

When testing your script, it's a good idea to start with simple tests and gradually increase the complexity of your tests. For example, if you are testing a script that creates a new user account in Active Directory, you might start with a test that creates a user with minimal properties and gradually increase the number of properties and complexity of the test data.

# Use Error Handling

Using error handling techniques such as try-catch blocks can help you handle errors that may occur during script execution. This helps prevent script failure and provides more informative error messages.

A try-catch block is a PowerShell construct that allows you to catch and handle errors that occur during script execution. Given below is an example of a try-catch block:

```
try {
    # Code that may cause an error goes here
}
catch {
    # Code to handle the error goes here
}
```

In the above given example, the code inside the try block is executed. If an error occurs, the script execution is halted, and the code inside the catch block is executed instead. This allows you to handle the error in a way that makes sense for your script.

# Use try-catch Block

Given below is an example of how to use a try-catch block in a script that creates a new user account in Active Directory:

```
# Define variables
$username = "jdoe"
$password = "P@ssw0rd"
$email = "jdoe@example.com"

try {
    # Check if user account exists
    Get-ADUser -Identity $username -ErrorAction Stop

    # User account already exists, throw an error
    throw "User account $username already exists"
}
catch {
    # User account does not exist, create a new account
    New-ADUser -Name $username -AccountPassword (ConvertTo-SecureString -AsPlainText -Force) -EmailAddress $email
}
```

In the above given sample program, we first define the variables that we need to create the user account. We then use a try block to check if the user account already exists. If the user account exists, we throw an error using the throw keyword. If the user account does not exist, we create a new user account using the New-ADUser cmdlet.

By using a try-catch block in this way, we can handle errors that may occur during script execution and prevent the script from failing.

# Writing Error-free Scripts

In addition to the above tips, there are some additional best practices that you can follow to ensure that your PowerShell scripts are error-free:
- Use comments: Use comments in your script to provide context and explain what

your code is doing. This makes your code more readable and easier to understand.

- Use indentation: Use indentation to make your code more readable and easier to understand. This helps you identify the structure of your script and makes it easier to follow.
- Use pipeline input: Use pipeline input to make your code more flexible and reusable. This allows you to pass data between cmdlets and functions, making it easier to create complex scripts.
- Use modules: Use modules to organize your code and make it easier to reuse. Modules allow you to encapsulate your code and distribute it as a package, making it easier for others to use your code.

By following these tips and best practices, you can write error-free PowerShell scripts that are efficient, readable, and easy to maintain.

# Edit PowerShell Scripts

## Understand the Script's Purpose

Before modifying a script, it's important to understand its purpose and how it works. This involves reviewing the script's code and identifying its intended functionality. You can accomplish this by reading through the script's comments, function names, and variable names.

For example, if you're working with a script that creates new user accounts in Active Directory, you should understand the script's workflow, what input parameters it expects, and how it interacts with Active Directory to create the user accounts.

## Make Copy of Original Script

Before making any changes to the script, it's important to create a copy of the original script. This ensures that you have a backup of the original code in case something goes wrong during the modification process.

## Use Version Control

Use version control to track your changes and collaborate with others. Version control allows you to track changes to your code over time and collaborate with others on your script. By using version control, you can easily revert to a previous version of your code if something goes wrong.

## Test Script Changes

After making changes to the script, test it on a small set of data or test environment. This helps you identify any errors or issues that need to be resolved before running the modified script in a production environment. In the event of modifying script, after making changes to the script, it's important to test your modifications to ensure that they work as intended. This involves testing your changes on a small set of data or a test environment to identify any issues or errors.

# Modify Existing Script

Modifying an existing script can be a challenging task, as you need to ensure that your changes do not introduce new errors or break the script's existing functionality. By following best practices and a structured approach, you can modify existing PowerShell scripts with confidence and avoid introducing errors.

## Procedure to Modify Script

To modify an existing script, follow these steps:
- Open the original script in your preferred text editor or integrated development environment (IDE).
- Make a copy of the original script and save it with a new name. This ensures that you have a backup of the original script in case something goes wrong during the modification process.
- Identify the section of the script that needs to be modified. In this example, we need to add a new property for the user's job title.
- Modify the script to include the new functionality. In this example, we added a new variable $title and included the -Title $title parameter when creating the new user account.
- Test the modified script on a small set of data or test environment to ensure that it works as intended.
- If the modified script works as intended, commit your changes to version control and deploy the modified script to a production environment.

## Sample Program

Using the example script from earlier section, let us say we want to modify it to include a new property for the user's job title. Given below is how we can modify the script:

# Define variables

```
$username = "jdoe"
$password = "P@ssw0rd"
$email = "jdoe@example.com"
$title = "Manager"

try {
    # Check if user account exists
    Get-ADUser -Identity $username -ErrorAction Stop

    # User account already exists, throw an error
    throw "User account $username already exists"
}
catch {
    # User account does not exist, create a new account
    New-ADUser -Name $username -AccountPassword (ConvertTo-
SecureString -AsPlainText -Force) -EmailAddress $email -Title $title
}
```

In this modified script, we have added a new variable $title, which represents the user's job title. We then include the -Title $title parameter when creating the new user account using the New-ADUser cmdlet.

To summarize, modifying existing PowerShell scripts requires a structured and organized approach that includes understanding the script's purpose, making a copy of the original script, using version control, identifying the specific section that needs to be modified, making your changes in a structured and organized way, and testing your changes on a small set of data or a test environment. By following these steps, you can modify existing PowerShell scripts with confidence and avoid introducing new errors or breaking the script's existing functionality.

# PowerShell Parameters

## Overveiw

PowerShell parameters can be declared using the "param" keyword, followed by a list of parameter names and their data types. You can also set default parameter values and specify whether a parameter is mandatory or optional.

When executing a PowerShell script or function, you can provide arguments for each parameter in a specific order, or use named parameters to provide values out of order. This allows you to customize the behavior of your script or function based on your specific needs. PowerShell parameters are a powerful feature that enables you to create scripts and functions that can be used in a variety of situations. By using parameters, you can create more flexible, adaptable, and reusable code that can save you time and effort in the long run.

Conceptually, there are two types of parameters in PowerShell:

## Positional Parameters

Positional parameters are a type of parameter in PowerShell that are defined by their position in a function or script call. In other words, the first parameter listed in the function or script definition is the first positional parameter, the second parameter is the second positional parameter, and so on. When calling a function or script that uses positional parameters, you can pass values for these parameters by specifying them in the correct order. For example, if a function has two positional parameters, you would pass the first value as the first argument and the second value as the second argument. It's important to keep the order of the positional parameters correct, or else the function or script may not work as intended.

## Named Parameters

Named parameters in PowerShell provide a more flexible way to pass arguments to a function or script. With named parameters, you can specify the parameter name followed by its value, which allows you to pass arguments in any order when calling the function or script. This is especially useful when a function or script has a large number of parameters, or when some of the parameters have default values that you don't need to specify. By using named parameters, you can make your code more readable and maintainable, and reduce the chances of errors caused by incorrect argument order.

# Using Parameters in Scripts

To use parameters in PowerShell, you simply include them in the command line or script, specifying their names and values, and PowerShell will use them as input for the operation. Given below is how to use parameters in PowerShell:

# Define Parameters in Script or Function

```
param(
  [Parameter(Mandatory=$true, Position=0)]
  [string]$Username,

  [Parameter(Mandatory=$true, Position=1)]
  [string]$Domain,

  [Parameter(Mandatory=$false)]
  [int]$Port = 80
)
```

This script defines three parameters: $Username (mandatory positional), $Domain (mandatory positional), and $Port (optional named with a default value of 80).

## Use Parameters within Script or Function

Write-Host "Connecting to domain $Domain using username $Username on port $Port"

This line uses the values of $Username, $Domain, and $Port to create a message.

## Call Script or Function with Parameters

For a script, save the code in a file (e.g., Connect.ps1), then call it with parameters:

.\Connect.ps1 -Username "JohnDoe" -Domain "example.com" -Port 443

For a function, define it in the current session or a module, then call it with parameters:

```
function Connect {
  # param block and script body as shown above
}
```

```
Connect -Username "JohnDoe" -Domain "example.com" -Port 443
```

Both examples pass the parameters $Username, $Domain, and $Port to the script or function. Note that the named parameters can be passed in any order.

# Arguments and Argument Parsing

Arguments in PowerShell refer to the values that are passed to a script, function, or cmdlet when it is called. These values are used to customize the behavior of the script, function, or cmdlet, and they are often associated with parameters. In PowerShell, arguments can be positional or named, just like parameters.

Concept-wise, arguments can be thought of as the input data that you provide when invoking a script or function, while parameters are the placeholders defined within the script or function to receive and handle those arguments. And, Argument parsing in PowerShell is the process of interpreting and assigning the provided arguments to the corresponding parameters in the script, function, or cmdlet. PowerShell has a built-in argument parser that automatically maps the arguments you pass to the correct parameters based on their names and positions.

Given below is a quick overview of how argument parsing works in PowerShell:

## Positional Arguments

Positional arguments in PowerShell are used to pass values to a script or function in a specific order. When a script or function is called with positional arguments, PowerShell maps those arguments to parameters based on their order. The first positional argument is assigned to the first positional parameter, the second argument to the second parameter, and so on. It's important to keep the order of positional arguments in mind when writing PowerShell scripts because if the arguments are not provided in the correct order, it can lead to unexpected behavior. Understanding how positional arguments work in PowerShell can help you create more efficient and effective scripts by allowing you to pass values to your functions or scripts in a predictable and consistent way.

## Named Arguments

In PowerShell, named arguments are a way to pass values to parameters in a specific order by specifying the parameter name along with its corresponding value. This allows you to provide arguments to a script or function in any order, which can be particularly useful when there are multiple parameters that need to be passed. PowerShell maps named arguments by searching for a parameter with the same name as the argument, regardless of their position in the argument list. By using named arguments, you can make your scripts more readable and easier to maintain, as well as reducing the risk of errors caused by incorrect ordering of arguments.

# Default Values

In PowerShell, you can specify default values for function parameters. If an argument is not provided for a parameter, PowerShell will automatically use the default value specified for that parameter. This can be useful for creating functions that are more flexible and can handle different scenarios without requiring the user to provide all the necessary arguments every time the function is called. If the user wants to override the default value, they can provide a value for the corresponding parameter when calling the function. Default values can also be used to avoid errors or unexpected behavior when a parameter is not provided or is invalid.

# Mandatory and Optional Parameters

In PowerShell, you can specify which parameters are mandatory and which ones are optional. When a parameter is marked as mandatory, it means that the user must provide a value for that parameter when running the script. If a mandatory parameter is not provided, PowerShell will raise an error and the script will not execute.

On the other hand, optional parameters do not require a value to be provided. If an optional parameter is not provided, the script will use its default value or behavior. This can be useful when you want to give the user the option to customize the behavior of the script without requiring them to provide values for all parameters.

# Type Conversion

Type conversion refers to the process of converting an argument or a variable from one data type to another. PowerShell's argument parser automatically converts arguments to the appropriate types based on the parameter's type definition. For example, if a parameter is defined as an integer, PowerShell will automatically convert any string argument to an integer.

However, if an argument cannot be converted to the required type, PowerShell will raise an error. This error can be handled by adding error handling code to the script. It is important to understand type conversion in PowerShell to ensure that your scripts execute correctly and to avoid errors caused by incompatible data types.

## Validation

PowerShell allows you to enforce validation rules for the parameters in your scripts, ensuring that they meet certain criteria. For instance, you can use PowerShell to validate that a numerical argument falls within a specific range, or that a string argument matches a specific pattern. If an argument fails validation, PowerShell will raise an error, letting you know that there is an issue with the input. This can help prevent errors and ensure that your script runs smoothly. By using parameter validation, you can make your PowerShell scripts more robust and reliable, reducing the likelihood of errors and making it easier to maintain and update your code.

# Implement and Parse Arguments

Let us consider a sample demonstration wherein we'll create a simple PowerShell script that takes two arguments as input: a number and an operation (either "square" or "cube"). The script will perform the specified operation on the number and display the result. This will demonstrate how to implement and parse arguments in PowerShell.

## Create MathOperation.ps1 Script

Create a new PowerShell script file (e.g., MathOperation.ps1) and add the following content:

```
param(
  [Parameter(Mandatory=$true, Position=0)]
  [int]$Number,

  [Parameter(Mandatory=$true, Position=1)]
  [ValidateSet("square", "cube")]
  [string]$Operation
)

function Perform-MathOperation {
    param(
        [int]$Number,
        [string]$Operation
```

```
    )

    switch ($Operation) {
        "square" { return $Number * $Number }
        "cube" { return $Number * $Number * $Number }
    }
}

$result = Perform-MathOperation -Number $Number -Operation $Operation
Write-Host "The $Operation of $Number is: $result"
```

This script defines two mandatory positional parameters: $Number (an integer) and $Operation (a string that must be either "square" or "cube"). It also defines a function Perform-MathOperation that takes these two parameters and performs the requested operation.

## Run Script with Arguments

Open a PowerShell console and navigate to the directory where you saved the MathOperation.ps1 script. Run the script with the desired arguments, for example:

```
.\MathOperation.ps1 5 square
```

This will output:

The square of 5 is: 25

## Using Named Arguments

```
.\MathOperation.ps1 -Number 3 -Operation cube
```

This will output:

The cube of 3 is: 27

In the above given sample program, PowerShell's built-in argument parser automatically maps the provided arguments (5 and square or 3 and cube) to the corresponding parameters ($Number and $Operation) in the script. The script then performs the specified operation and displays the result.

# Debugging PowerShell

Debugging in PowerShell involves using various techniques to identify and resolve issues or errors in your scripts or functions. One way to debug PowerShell scripts is to use built-in cmdlets like Get-Variable, which allows you to check the value of variables at various stages of your script. Another technique is to leverage the Write-Host or Write-Verbose cmdlets, which can help you track the flow of your script and output debug information. Additionally, PowerShell allows you to set breakpoints in an Integrated Scripting Environment (ISE) or code editor like Visual Studio Code, which can help you pause your script at specific points to inspect variables or step through the code. These techniques can help you quickly and efficiently debug your PowerShell scripts and functions.

Here are different techniques for debugging in PowerShell with examples:

## Write-Host and Write-Verbose

Write-Host is a cmdlet that can be used to display output to the console or host window during script execution. This cmdlet is commonly used to display informational messages, error messages, or warning messages to the user. Write-Host can also be used to output variable values or other data to the console.

Write-Verbose is another cmdlet that can be used to output diagnostic information during script execution. However, Write-Verbose is specifically designed to output verbose messages, which are used to provide detailed information about what the script is doing at each step. Verbose messages are useful for debugging and troubleshooting scripts, as they can help identify issues or errors that may be occurring during execution. To see verbose output, the script must be run with the -Verbose parameter.

## Sample Program: Write-Host and Write-Verbose

```powershell
Copy code
$numbers = 1..10
```

```powershell
foreach ($number in $numbers) {
    Write-Host "Processing number: $number"
    $result = $number * 2
    Write-Host "Result: $result`n"
}
```

## Set-PSBreakpoint

The Set-PSBreakpoint cmdlet is an important tool for debugging PowerShell scripts. By setting breakpoints at specific points in your code, you can take control of the script's execution and analyze its behavior. When a breakpoint is hit, the script will pause, and you can use PowerShell's interactive debugging features to examine the state of the script's variables and objects. You can step through the code one line at a time, or continue the script's execution until the next breakpoint is hit. This allows you to identify and fix bugs in your script more quickly and efficiently. The Set-PSBreakpoint cmdlet also allows you to set conditions for when a breakpoint should be triggered, providing even more control over your script's behavior during debugging.

## Sample Program: Set-PSBreakpoint

Save the following script as MultiplyNumbers.ps1:

```powershell
powershell
Copy code
$numbers = 1..10
foreach ($number in $numbers) {
    $result = $number * 2
    Write-Host "$number * 2 = $result"
}
```

In the PowerShell console, set a breakpoint on line 3:

Set-PSBreakpoint -Script .\MultiplyNumbers.ps1 -Line 3

Run the script:

.\MultiplyNumbers.ps1

When the breakpoint is hit, PowerShell will pause execution and display a debugging prompt. You can use the following commands to navigate through the script:

- s or step: Step into the next line
- v or stepover: Step over the next line
- c or continue: Continue execution until the next breakpoint or the script ends
- q or quit: Stop debugging and exit the script

# CHAPTER 7: WINDOWS MANAGEMENT WITH POWERSHELL

# Managing Files, Folders, and Drives

PowerShell is a versatile tool for managing files, folders, and drives. With its wide range of cmdlets, users can perform various operations like creating, moving, renaming, deleting, and copying files and folders. PowerShell also allows users to manage drives, such as creating, formatting, and assigning drive letters. By using PowerShell's scripting capabilities, users can automate repetitive tasks and perform complex operations with ease. In this guide, we'll cover some practical examples of using PowerShell to manage files, folders, and drives to help users become more efficient in their daily tasks.

## Navigating File System

To change the current directory, use the Set-Location cmdlet (or its alias cd):

Set-Location -Path C:\Users

To display the current directory, use the Get-Location cmdlet (or its alias pwd):

Get-Location

## Creating and Removing Directories

To create a new directory, use the New-Item cmdlet with -ItemType Directory:

New-Item -Path "C:\Example" -ItemType Directory

To remove a directory, use the Remove-Item cmdlet (or its alias rm). To remove a non-empty directory, use the -Recurse switch:

Remove-Item -Path "C:\Example" -Recurse

## Creating, Reading, and Editing Files

To create a new file, use the New-Item cmdlet with -ItemType File:

New-Item -Path "C:\Example\test.txt" -ItemType File

To read the contents of a file, use the Get-Content cmdlet (or its alias gc):

Get-Content -Path "C:\Example\test.txt"

To write to a file, use the Set-Content cmdlet (or its alias sc). This will overwrite the file's contents:

Set-Content -Path "C:\Example\test.txt" -Value "Hello, World!"

To append data to a file, use the Add-Content cmdlet:

Add-Content -Path "C:\Example\test.txt" -Value "This is a new line."

To replace text in a file, use the Get-Content cmdlet to read the file, then pipe the output to the ForEach-Object cmdlet to perform the replacement, and finally use the Set-Content cmdlet to save the changes:

```
(Get-Content -Path "C:\Example\test.txt") |
ForEach-Object { $_ -replace "World", "PowerShell" } |
Set-Content -Path "C:\Example\test.txt"
```

# Copying, Moving, and Renaming Files and Folders

To copy a file or folder, use the Copy-Item cmdlet (or its alias cp):

Copy-Item -Path "C:\Example\test.txt" -Destination "C:\Example\test_copy.txt"

To move a file or folder, use the Move-Item cmdlet (or its alias mv):

Move-Item -Path "C:\Example\test.txt" -Destination "C:\Example\test_moved.txt"

To rename a file or folder, use the Rename-Item cmdlet (or its alias ren):

Rename-Item -Path "C:\Example\test.txt" -NewName "test_renamed.txt"

# Working with Drives

To list available drives, use the Get-PSDrive cmdlet:

```
Get-PSDrive
```

To change the current drive, use the Set-Location cmdlet (or its alias cd):

```
Set-Location -Path "D:"
```

To get information about a specific drive, use the `Get-Volume` cmdlet:

```
Get-Volume -DriveLetter D
```

# Filtering and Sorting Items

To list items in a directory, use the Get-ChildItem cmdlet (or its alias ls or dir). You can filter the results using the -Filter, -Include, or -Exclude parameters:

```
Get-ChildItem -Path "C:\Example" -Filter "*.txt"
```

To list items recursively, use the -Recurse switch:

```
Get-ChildItem -Path "C:\Example" -Recurse
```

To sort items, use the Sort-Object cmdlet (or its alias sort). For example, to sort items by their last write time:

```
Get-ChildItem -Path "C:\Example" | Sort-Object -Property LastWriteTime
```

# Working with File and Folder Attributes

To get the attributes of a file or folder, use the Get-Item cmdlet and access the Attributes property:

```
(Get-Item -Path "C:\Example\test.txt").Attributes
```

To set attributes, use the Set-ItemProperty cmdlet. For example, to set a file as read-only:

```
Set-ItemProperty -Path "C:\Example\test.txt" -Name Attributes -Value ([System.IO.FileAttributes]::ReadOnly)
```

To remove the read-only attribute, use bitwise operations:

```
$attributes = (Get-Item -Path "C:\Example\test.txt").Attributes
$attributes = $attributes -band (-bnot [System.IO.FileAttributes]::ReadOnly)
Set-ItemProperty -Path "C:\Example\test.txt" -Name Attributes -Value $attributes
```

## Calculating Folder Size

To calculate the size of a folder, use the Get-ChildItem cmdlet to list all files recursively and then use the Measure-Object cmdlet (or its alias measure) to sum their lengths:

```
$folderSize = (Get-ChildItem -Path "C:\Example" -Recurse -File | Measure-Object -Property Length -Sum).Sum
Write-Host "Folder size: $($folderSize / 1MB) MB"
```

These examples showcase how PowerShell can be used to manage files, folders, and drives. You can combine these cmdlets and techniques to create more complex scripts and automate file management tasks according to your needs.

# Working with the Windows Registry

The Windows Registry is an essential component of the Windows operating system that enables users and applications to store and retrieve system and application configuration data. It is a complex hierarchical database that contains a vast array of settings and options organized into a tree-like structure. The registry is made up of five primary hives, which are responsible for storing various types of system and application data.

PowerShell, a powerful command-line interface and scripting language, provides an extensive set of built-in cmdlets to manage and work with the Windows Registry. These cmdlets enable users to perform a variety of tasks, such as adding, modifying, and deleting registry keys and values, querying registry data, and exporting and importing registry settings. Additionally, PowerShell also supports the creation of custom scripts and modules, making it easier for users to automate complex registry management tasks. Overall, PowerShell's ability to work with the Windows Registry makes it a valuable tool for system administrators and power users.

## Navigating the Registry

PowerShell treats the registry like a file system, with the HKLM: and HKCU: drives representing the HKEY_LOCAL_MACHINE and HKEY_CURRENT_USER hives, respectively. You can use the Set-Location, Get-Location, and Get-ChildItem cmdlets to navigate the registry:

```
Set-Location -Path "HKLM:\SOFTWARE"
Get-ChildItem
```

## Reading Registry Keys and Values

To read a registry key, use the Get-Item cmdlet:

```
Get-Item -Path "HKLM:\SOFTWARE\Microsoft\Windows\CurrentVersion"
```

To read a registry value, use the Get-ItemProperty cmdlet:

```
Get-ItemProperty -Path
"HKLM:\SOFTWARE\Microsoft\Windows\CurrentVersion" -Name
"ProgramFilesDir"
```

## Creating and Removing Registry Keys

To create a new registry key, use the New-Item cmdlet:

```
New-Item -Path "HKCU:\Software\ExampleKey"
```

To remove a registry key, use the Remove-Item cmdlet:

```
Remove-Item -Path "HKCU:\Software\ExampleKey"
```

## Creating, Modifying, and Removing Registry Values

To create or modify a registry value, use the Set-ItemProperty cmdlet:

```
Set-ItemProperty -Path "HKCU:\Software\ExampleKey" -Name
"ExampleValue" -Value "PowerShell" -Type String
```

To remove a registry value, use the Remove-ItemProperty cmdlet:

```
Remove-ItemProperty -Path "HKCU:\Software\ExampleKey" -Name
"ExampleValue"
```

## Exporting and Importing Registry Keys

To export a registry key, use the Export-RegistryFile cmdlet:

```
Export-RegistryFile -Path "HKCU:\Software\ExampleKey" -Destination
"C:\Example\ExampleKey.reg"
```

To import a registry key, use the Import-RegistryFile cmdlet:

```
Import-RegistryFile -Path "C:\Example\ExampleKey.reg"
```

## Searching Registry

To search the registry for specific keys or values, use the Get-ChildItem cmdlet with the -Recurse switch and pipe the output to the Where-Object cmdlet:

```
Get-ChildItem -Path "HKLM:\SOFTWARE" -Recurse | Where-Object {
$_.Name -like "*Example*" }
```

# Managing Processes, Services, and Event Logs

PowerShell is a powerful tool for managing Windows systems, and administrators must possess the skill of managing processes, services, and event logs using this tool to ensure the smooth functioning of their systems. With PowerShell, administrators can easily track and analyze system processes, manage and configure system services, and monitor event logs for any errors or security issues. In this section, we will explore some practical examples of how to use PowerShell to manage these crucial system components and maintain the overall health of your Windows systems.

# Processes

To list all running processes, use the Get-Process cmdlet (or its alias gps):

Get-Process

To filter processes by name, use the -Name parameter:

Get-Process -Name "notepad"

To start a new process, use the Start-Process cmdlet (or its alias saps):

Start-Process -FilePath "notepad.exe"

To stop a process, use the Stop-Process cmdlet (or its alias kill). You can specify the process using its ID or name:

Stop-Process -Id 12345
or
Stop-Process -Name "notepad"

# Services

To list all services, use the Get-Service cmdlet:

et-Service

To filter services by name or display name, use the -Name parameter or pipe the output to the Where-Object cmdlet (or its alias where):

```
Get-Service -Name "wuauserv"
```

or

```
Get-Service | Where-Object { $_.DisplayName -like "*Windows Update*" }
```

To start a service, use the Start-Service cmdlet:

```
Start-Service -Name "wuauserv"
```

To stop a service, use the Stop-Service cmdlet:

```
Stop-Service -Name "wuauserv"
```

To set a service's startup type, use the Set-Service cmdlet:

```
Set-Service -Name "wuauserv" -StartupType "Manual"
```

# Event Logs

Managing Event Logs involves working with the built-in cmdlets designed for interacting with the Windows Event Log system. This system records events from various sources, such as applications, security auditing processes, and the operating system itself.

## Viewing Available Event Logs

To list all available event logs, use the Get-EventLog cmdlet with the -List parameter:

```
Get-EventLog -List
```

## Reading Event Logs

To read events from a specific log, use the Get-EventLog cmdlet and specify the log name with the -LogName parameter:

```
Get-EventLog -LogName Application
```

You can limit the number of events returned using the -Newest parameter:

```
Get-EventLog -LogName Application -Newest 10
```

# Filtering Event Logs

To filter events based on specific criteria, you can use the Where-Object cmdlet (or its alias where). For example, to retrieve only error events:

```
Get-EventLog -LogName Application | Where-Object { $_.EntryType -eq 'Error' }
```

Or to filter events by a specific source:

```
Get-EventLog -LogName Application | Where-Object { $_.Source -eq 'YourSource' }
```

# Searching for Specific Event IDs

To search for events with a specific Event ID, use the -InstanceId parameter:

```
Get-EventLog -LogName Application -InstanceId 1000
```

# Exporting Event Logs

To export events to a CSV or XML file, you can use the Export-Csv or ConvertTo-Xml cmdlets, respectively:

```
Get-EventLog -LogName Application -Newest 100 | Export-Csv -Path "C:\Example\EventLogs.csv"
```

```
$events = Get-EventLog -LogName Application -Newest 100
$eventsXml = $events | ConvertTo-Xml
$eventsXml.Save("C:\Example\EventLogs.xml")
```

# Clearing Event Logs

To clear an event log, use the Clear-EventLog cmdlet and specify the log name with the -

LogName parameter:

Clear-EventLog -LogName Application

## Creating and Managing Custom Event Logs

To create a new custom event log, use the New-EventLog cmdlet:

New-EventLog -LogName "CustomLog" -Source "MyApplication"

To write events to a custom event log, use the Write-EventLog cmdlet:

Write-EventLog -LogName "CustomLog" -Source "MyApplication" -
EntryType Information -EventId 1 -Message "This is a test event."

# Managing Scheduled Tasks

PowerShell is a powerful tool for managing Windows Scheduled Tasks. By using cmdlets specifically designed for interacting with the Task Scheduler, users can easily create, modify, and remove tasks. The Task Scheduler is a built-in feature of Windows that allows for automation of tasks, such as running programs or scripts, on a set schedule or under specific conditions. PowerShell's ability to interact with the Task Scheduler allows for efficient management of these tasks, such as enabling or disabling them, setting triggers and actions, and configuring settings like priority and credentials. With PowerShell, managing Windows Scheduled Tasks is streamlined and easy, making automation a breeze.

Given below is a doable solution on how to work with Scheduled Tasks using PowerShell:

## Listing Scheduled Tasks

To list all scheduled tasks, use the Get-ScheduledTask cmdlet:

Get-ScheduledTask

## Getting Information Of a Specific Task

To get information about a specific task, use the Get-ScheduledTask cmdlet with the -TaskName parameter:

```
Get-ScheduledTask -TaskName "YourTaskName"
```

# Creating New Scheduled Task

To create a new scheduled task, you need to define an action, a trigger, and then register the task.

First, create the action using the New-ScheduledTaskAction cmdlet:

```
$action = New-ScheduledTaskAction -Execute "C:\Path\To\YourScript.ps1"
```

Next, create a trigger using the New-ScheduledTaskTrigger cmdlet. For example, to create a daily trigger at 6:00 AM:

```
$trigger = New-ScheduledTaskTrigger -Daily -At 6am
```

Finally, register the task using the Register-ScheduledTask cmdlet:

```
Register-ScheduledTask -TaskName "MyScheduledTask" -Action $action -Trigger $trigger
```

# Updating Existing Scheduled Task

To update an existing task, first, get the task using the Get-ScheduledTask cmdlet:

```
$task = Get-ScheduledTask -TaskName "YourTaskName"
```

Then, update the properties you want to change, such as the action or trigger. For example, to change the action to execute a different script:

```
$task.Actions[0].Execute = "C:\Path\To\NewScript.ps1"
```

Finally, update the task using the Set-ScheduledTask cmdlet:

```
Set-ScheduledTask -TaskName "YourTaskName" -TaskObject $task
```

# Running Scheduled Task Manually

To run a scheduled task manually, use the Start-ScheduledTask cmdlet:

```
Start-ScheduledTask -TaskName "YourTaskName"
```

# Stopping Running Scheduled Task

To stop a running scheduled task, use the Stop-ScheduledTask cmdlet:

```
Stop-ScheduledTask -TaskName "YourTaskName"
```

# Enabling and Disabling Scheduled Task

To enable or disable a scheduled task, use the Enable-ScheduledTask or Disable-ScheduledTask cmdlet, respectively:

```
Enable-ScheduledTask -TaskName "YourTaskName"
```

Or

```
Disable-ScheduledTask -TaskName "YourTaskName"
```

# Removing Scheduled Task

To remove a scheduled task, use the Unregister-ScheduledTask cmdlet:

```
Unregister-ScheduledTask -TaskName "YourTaskName" -Confirm:$false
```

To summarize, these cmdlets allow users to create, modify, and delete scheduled tasks, as well as retrieve information about them. PowerShell also allows for the configuration of task settings such as triggers, actions, and conditions. With PowerShell, users can easily automate the management of scheduled tasks, making it a powerful tool for system administrators and IT professionals.

# CHAPTER 8: ACTIVE DIRECTORY MANAGEMENT

# Active Directory PowerShell Module

The Active Directory (AD) PowerShell module is a collection of cmdlets that enables administrators to manage Active Directory Domain Services (AD DS) and Active Directory Lightweight Directory Services (AD LDS) using PowerShell. The module offers a powerful and efficient way to perform various tasks related to user, group, computer, and organizational unit (OU) management, as well as tasks related to Active Directory schema, trusts, and replication.

The AD PowerShell module is included in the Remote Server Administration Tools (RSAT) package on client operating systems like Windows 10 and Windows 11. On Windows Server, it can be installed via the "RSAT-AD-PowerShell" feature using the Add-WindowsFeature cmdlet or the Server Manager.

Once installed, you can load the module with the Import-Module cmdlet:

Import-Module ActiveDirectory

Here are some key aspects and cmdlets of the Active Directory PowerShell module:

## Discoverability

Cmdlets in the AD module follow the standard verb-noun naming convention, making it easier to discover and use them. For instance, Get-ADUser, Get-ADGroup, and Get-ADComputer are used to retrieve user, group, and computer objects, respectively.

You can use Get-Command with the '-Module ActiveDirectory' parameter to list all cmdlets available in the module:

Get-Command -Module ActiveDirectory

## Managing Users

The AD module provides cmdlets to create, modify, and remove user accounts, as well as to manage user properties and group memberships.

Examples include:
- New-ADUser: Create a new user account.
- Set-ADUser: Modify properties of an existing user account.
- Get-ADUser: Retrieve user account details.

- Remove-ADUser: Delete a user account.
- Add-ADGroupMember: Add a user to a group.
- Remove-ADGroupMember: Remove a user from a group.

## Managing Groups

You can use the AD module to manage group objects and their properties. Some cmdlets for group management include:
- New-ADGroup: Create a new group.
- Set-ADGroup: Modify group properties.
- Get-ADGroup: Retrieve group details.
- Remove-ADGroup: Delete a group.
- Get-ADGroupMember: List members of a group.

## Managing Computers

The module also offers cmdlets for managing computer accounts in Active Directory, such as:
- New-ADComputer: Create a new computer account.
- Set-ADComputer: Modify computer account properties.
- Get-ADComputer: Retrieve computer account details.
- Remove-ADComputer: Delete a computer account.
- Move-ADObject: Move a computer account to a different OU.

## Managing Organizational Units (OUs)

Organizational units are used to organize and manage Active Directory objects. The AD module includes cmdlets to work with OUs:
- New-ADOrganizationalUnit: Create a new OU.
- Set-ADOrganizationalUnit: Modify OU properties.
- Get-ADOrganizationalUnit: Retrieve OU details.
- Remove-ADOrganizationalUnit: Delete an OU.

# Installing Active Directory Module

To manage Active Directory (AD) users, groups, and computers using PowerShell, you'll need to install the Active Directory module for PowerShell first. You can install it by adding the "RSAT-AD-PowerShell" feature on Windows Server or the "RSAT-AD-Tools" feature on Windows 10/11.

Installing the Active Directory module on Windows Server:

```
Install-WindowsFeature -Name RSAT-AD-PowerShell
```

To Installing the Active Directory module on Windows 10/11:

```
Add-WindowsCapability -Online -Name Rsat.ActiveDirectory.DS-
LDS.Tools~~~~0.0.1.0
```

Import the Active Directory module:

```
Import-Module ActiveDirectory
```

Now, you can use various cmdlets to manage AD users, groups, and computers. Here are some examples:

# Manage AD Users

To manage Active Directory users, you can create a new user account. This involves specifying the user's details such as name, username, password, and group memberships using appropriate tools.

*Create a new user:*

```
New-ADUser -Name "John Doe" -GivenName "John" -Surname "Doe" -
SamAccountName "jdoe" -UserPrincipalName "jdoe@yourdomain.com" -
AccountPassword (ConvertTo-SecureString "P@ssw0rd" -AsPlainText -Force)
-Enabled $true
```

*Get a user:*

```
Get-ADUser -Identity "jdoe" -Properties *
```

*Modify a user's attribute:*

```
Set-ADUser -Identity "jdoe" -Title "IT Support Specialist"
```

*Reset a user's password:*

Set-ADAccountPassword -Identity "jdoe" -NewPassword (ConvertTo-SecureString "NewP@ssw0rd" -AsPlainText -Force)

*Disable or enable a user account:*

Disable-ADAccount -Identity "jdoe"
Enable-ADAccount -Identity "jdoe"

*Remove a user:*

Remove-ADUser -Identity "jdoe"

# Manage AD Groups

One way to manage AD groups is through the Active Directory Users and Computers (ADUC) tool. From ADUC, you can create, modify, and delete groups, add or remove members, and set group permissions.

*Create a new group:*

New-ADGroup -Name "IT Support" -GroupScope Global -GroupCategory Security -Path "OU=Groups,DC=yourdomain,DC=com"

*Get a group:*

Get-ADGroup -Identity "IT Support"

*Add a user to a group:*

Add-ADGroupMember -Identity "IT Support" -Members "jdoe"

*Remove a user from a group:*

Remove-ADGroupMember -Identity "IT Support" -Members "jdoe" -Confirm:$false

*Remove a group:*

Remove-ADGroup -Identity "IT Support"

# Manage Computer

Managing computers in the Active Directory (AD) module involves configuring computer accounts, group policies, and access control. It enables administrators to centrally manage and maintain computer resources, deploy software, and enforce security policies.

*Create a new computer account:*
To create a new computer account in the Active Directory, use the New-ADComputer cmdlet:

New-ADComputer -Name "Computer01" -SamAccountName "Computer01" -Path "OU=Computers,DC=example,DC=com"

This will create a new computer account named "Computer01" in the "Computers" organizational unit (OU) within the "example.com" domain.

*Get information about a computer account:*
To retrieve information about a specific computer account, use the Get-ADComputer cmdlet:

Get-ADComputer -Identity "Computer01" -Properties *

This will display all properties for the "Computer01" computer account.

*Update computer account properties:*
To update a property of a computer account, use the Set-ADComputer cmdlet:

Set-ADComputer -Identity "Computer01" -Description "This is a test computer"

This will set the description of the "Computer01" computer account to "This is a test computer."

*Move a computer account to a different OU:*
To move a computer account to another OU, use the Move-ADObject cmdlet:

$computer = Get-ADComputer -Identity "Computer01"
Move-ADObject -Identity $computer -TargetPath
"OU=NewComputers,DC=example,DC=com"

This will move the "Computer01" computer account from its current OU to the "NewComputers" OU.

*Disable or enable a computer account:*
To disable or enable a computer account, use the Disable-ADAccount or Enable-ADAccount cmdlets:

Disable-ADAccount -Identity "Computer01"
Enable-ADAccount -Identity "Computer01"

These cmdlets will disable and enable the "Computer01" computer account, respectively.

*Remove a computer account:*
To delete a computer account, use the Remove-ADComputer cmdlet:

Remove-ADComputer -Identity "Computer01" -Confirm:$false

This will delete the "Computer01" computer account without prompting for confirmation.

# Manage Organizational Units (OUs)

Organizational Units (OUs) are a fundamental component of Active Directory, which is a hierarchical database used to manage resources in a Windows domain network. OUs are used to group and organize objects like users, groups, and computers, enabling you to delegate administrative control over these objects to specific users or groups. PowerShell provides a set of cmdlets for managing OUs, allowing administrators to automate tasks such as creating new OUs, modifying their attributes, moving objects between OUs, and deleting OUs. By leveraging PowerShell's scripting capabilities, administrators can streamline routine management tasks, improve consistency, and reduce the likelihood of errors.

Assuming you have the AD module installed, below is a step-by-step solution on how to practically manage OUs using PowerShell:

*Import the Active Directory module:*
Before using the AD module, you need to import it into your PowerShell session:

**Import-Module ActiveDirectory**

*Create a new OU:*
To create a new OU in the Active Directory, use the New-ADOrganizationalUnit cmdlet:

**New-ADOrganizationalUnit -Name "NewOU" -Path "OU=Computers,DC=example,DC=com"**

This will create a new OU named "NewOU" within the "Computers" OU of the "example.com" domain.

*Get information about an OU:*
To retrieve information about a specific OU, use the Get-ADOrganizationalUnit cmdlet:

**Get-ADOrganizationalUnit -Identity "OU=NewOU,OU=Computers,DC=example,DC=com"**

This will display information about the "NewOU" OU.

*Rename an OU:*
To rename an OU, use the Rename-ADObject cmdlet:

**Rename-ADObject -Identity**

"OU=NewOU,OU=Computers,DC=example,DC=com" -NewName "NewOU2"

This will rename the "NewOU" OU to "NewOU2".

*Move an OU:*
To move an OU to a different parent OU, use the Move-ADObject cmdlet:

Move-ADObject -Identity
"OU=NewOU2,OU=Computers,DC=example,DC=com" -TargetPath
"OU=NewParentOU,DC=example,DC=com"

This will move the "NewOU2" OU to the "NewParentOU" OU.

*Remove an OU:*
To remove an OU, use the Remove-ADOrganizationalUnit cmdlet:

Remove-ADOrganizationalUnit -Identity
"OU=NewOU2,OU=NewParentOU,DC=example,DC=com" -Confirm:$false

This will remove the "NewOU2" OU without prompting for confirmation.

These examples demonstrate how to use PowerShell for managing OUs in the Active Directory. By leveraging these cmdlets, you can efficiently create, modify, move, and delete OUs to organize and manage objects in your Active Directory environment.

# Manage Group Policy Objects (GPOs)

Group Policy Objects (GPOs) are a critical component of Active Directory that enables administrators to manage and enforce policies on users and computers. GPOs contain configuration settings that can be applied to specific users, groups, or computers within an Active Directory domain. PowerShell, a powerful scripting language and command-line tool, offers a set of cmdlets that allow administrators to manage GPOs efficiently. With PowerShell, you can create new GPOs, modify existing ones, link them to organizational units, and unlink them when they are no longer needed. PowerShell's GPO management capabilities make it an essential tool for Active Directory administrators who need to manage large and complex environments.

Assuming you have the AD module installed, let us learn how to practically manage GPOs using PowerShell:

*Import the Group Policy module:*
Before using the Group Policy module, you need to import it into your PowerShell session:

```
Import-Module GroupPolicy
```

*Create a new GPO:*
To create a new GPO in the Active Directory, use the New-GPO cmdlet:

```
New-GPO -Name "NewGPO"
```

This will create a new GPO named "NewGPO".

*Get information about a GPO:*
To retrieve information about a specific GPO, use the Get-GPO cmdlet:

```
Get-GPO -Name "NewGPO"
```

This will display information about the "NewGPO" GPO.

*Modify a GPO:*
To modify the settings of a GPO, use the Set-GPRegistryValue, Set-GPPermission, or Set-GPRegistryPolicy cmdlets, depending on the type of setting you want to modify. For example, to modify a registry value in a GPO:

```
Set-GPRegistryValue -Name "NewGPO" -Key
"HKCU:\Software\Microsoft\Windows\CurrentVersion\Policies\Explorer" -
ValueName "NoDriveTypeAutoRun" -Type DWORD -Value 0x000000FF
```

This will set the "NoDriveTypeAutoRun" registry value in the "NewGPO" GPO to 0x000000FF.

*Link a GPO:*
To link a GPO to a domain, site, or organizational unit (OU), use the New-GPLink cmdlet:

```
New-GPLink -Name "NewGPO" -Target
```

"OU=Computers,DC=example,DC=com"

This will link the "NewGPO" GPO to the "Computers" OU of the "example.com" domain.

*Unlink a GPO:*
To unlink a GPO from a domain, site, or OU, use the Remove-GPLink cmdlet:

Remove-GPLink -Name "NewGPO" -Target "OU=Computers,DC=example,DC=com"

This will unlink the "NewGPO" GPO from the "Computers" OU.

*Remove a GPO:*
To remove a GPO, use the Remove-GPO cmdlet:

Remove-GPO -Name "NewGPO" -Confirm:$false

This will remove the "NewGPO" GPO without prompting for confirmation.

These examples demonstrate how to use PowerShell for managing GPOs in the Active Directory. By leveraging these cmdlets, you can efficiently create, modify, link, and unlink GPOs to apply configuration settings to users and computers in your Active Directory environment.

# Managing Active Directory Sites and Replication

Active Directory Sites and Replication are used to ensure that Active Directory information is available and up-to-date across multiple domain controllers in different locations. PowerShell provides cmdlets for managing sites, subnets, and replication connections, allowing you to create, modify, and remove them.

Assuming you have the AD module installed, let us learn how to practically manage Active Directory Sites and Replication using PowerShell:

*Import the Active Directory module:*
Before using the AD module, you need to import it into your PowerShell session:

Import-Module ActiveDirectory

### Create a new site:

To create a new site in the Active Directory, use the New-ADSite cmdlet:

New-ADSite -Name "NewSite"

This will create a new site named "NewSite".

### Get information about a site:

To retrieve information about a specific site, use the Get-ADSite cmdlet:

Get-ADSite -Identity "NewSite"

This will display information about the "NewSite" site.

### Modify a site:

To modify the settings of a site, use the Set-ADSite cmdlet:

Set-ADSite -Identity "NewSite" -Description "This is a new site"

This will set the description of the "NewSite" site to "This is a new site".

### Create a new subnet:

To create a new subnet within a site, use the New-ADSubnet cmdlet:

New-ADSubnet -Name "NewSubnet" -Site "NewSite" -Location "New Location" -IPv4Subnet "192.168.0.0/24"

This will create a new subnet named "NewSubnet" with an IPv4 subnet mask of "192.168.0.0/24" in the "NewSite" site with a location of "New Location".

### Get information about a subnet:

To retrieve information about a specific subnet, use the Get-ADSubnet cmdlet:

Get-ADSubnet -Identity "NewSubnet"

This will display information about the "NewSubnet" subnet.

*Modify a subnet:*
To modify the settings of a subnet, use the Set-ADSubnet cmdlet:

Set-ADSubnet -Identity "NewSubnet" -Location "New Location 2"

This will set the location of the "NewSubnet" subnet to "New Location 2".

*Create a new replication connection:*
To create a new replication connection between domain controllers, use the New-ADReplicationConnection cmdlet:

New-ADReplicationConnection -SourceServer "DC1" -DestinationServer "DC2"

This will create a new replication connection between "DC1" and "DC2".

*Get information about a replication connection:*
To retrieve information about a specific replication connection, use the Get-ADReplicationConnection cmdlet:

Get-ADReplicationConnection -SourceServer "DC1" -DestinationServer "DC2"

This will display information about the replication connection between "DC1" and "DC2".

*Remove a replication connection:*
To remove a replication connection, use the Remove-ADReplicationConnection cmdlet:

Remove-ADReplicationConnection -SourceServer "DC1" -DestinationServer "DC2" -Confirm:$false

This will remove the replication connection between "DC1" and "DC2" without prompting for confirmation.

These examples demonstrate how to use PowerShell for managing Active Directory Sites and Replication. By leveraging these cmdlets, you can efficiently create, modify, and remove sites, subnets, and replication connections to ensure that Active Directory information is available and up-to-date across multiple domain controllers in different locations.

# CHAPTER 9: POWERSHELL REMOTING

# PowerShell Remoting

PowerShell Remoting is a powerful feature of PowerShell, a scripting language and automation framework designed specifically for Windows environments. It enables administrators and developers to execute PowerShell commands and scripts on remote machines, allowing them to manage multiple systems efficiently and securely.

PowerShell Remoting can be broken down into several key components and ideas:

## Windows Remote Management (WinRM)

PowerShell Remoting relies on WinRM, a Microsoft implementation of the WS-Management protocol, which is an industry-standard SOAP-based protocol for managing systems. WinRM allows communication between remote systems using HTTP or HTTPS, providing a secure foundation for PowerShell Remoting.

## PowerShell Sessions (PSSessions)

A PSSession represents a persistent connection to a remote machine. Using PSSessions, you can execute multiple commands on the remote system without having to re-establish the connection each time. PSSessions can be created using the New-PSSession cmdlet and managed using cmdlets like Enter-PSSession, Exit-PSSession, and Remove-PSSession.

## Implicit Remoting

Implicit Remoting allows you to import remote PowerShell modules into your local session, effectively making remote cmdlets available as if they were local. This can be done using the Import-PSSession cmdlet. Implicit Remoting allows you to work with remote systems seamlessly, without having to enter an interactive session.

## Security and Authentication

PowerShell Remoting provides several authentication mechanisms to ensure secure communication between the local and remote systems, such as Kerberos, NTLM, and CredSSP. Additionally, you can configure SSL for encryption and certificate-based authentication. It is essential to configure the appropriate authentication and security settings to protect sensitive information and prevent unauthorized access.

## Execution Policy

PowerShell has a built-in feature called Execution Policy, which determines the level of security for running scripts. You need to ensure that the execution policy on both the local and remote systems is set appropriately to allow running remote scripts. Common execution policies include Restricted, AllSigned, RemoteSigned, and Unrestricted.

## Remote Commands and Scriptblocks

When using PowerShell Remoting, you can execute individual commands or scriptblocks on remote systems. A scriptblock is a collection of PowerShell commands enclosed in curly braces {}. You can execute remote commands using cmdlets like Invoke-Command and supply a scriptblock or a file containing a script.

PowerShell Remoting is an essential tool for managing multiple systems in a Windows environment. It simplifies remote administration, enhances automation capabilities, and provides a secure method for executing PowerShell commands and scripts on remote machines. Understanding these core concepts will help you effectively utilize PowerShell Remoting in your administration and automation tasks.

# One-to-One Remoting

In PowerShell Remoting, there are two primary communication patterns: One-to-One and One-to-Many. One-to-One involves connecting to a single remote machine, while One-to-Many refers to connecting to multiple remote machines simultaneously.

One-to-One Remoting is the simplest form of PowerShell Remoting, where you execute commands on a single remote machine. There are two main ways to perform One-to-One Remoting: using an interactive session or invoking commands.

## Interactive Session

An interactive session allows you to establish a connection to a remote machine and execute commands as if you were directly logged into that machine. To create an interactive session, use the following steps:

Open PowerShell on your local machine.

Run Enter-PSSession cmdlet followed by the remote machine's name or IP address:

**Enter-PSSession -ComputerName RemoteComputer**

Replace RemoteComputer with the remote machine's name or IP address.

You are now in an interactive session with the remote machine. Execute any PowerShell commands as if you were on the remote machine itself.

To exit the interactive session, run Exit-PSSession.

## Invoking Commands

You can execute commands on a remote machine without entering an interactive session using the Invoke-Command cmdlet. To do this, follow these steps:

Open PowerShell on your local machine.

Run the Invoke-Command cmdlet, specifying the remote machine's name or IP address, and the command or scriptblock to execute:

```
Invoke-Command -ComputerName RemoteComputer -ScriptBlock { Get-Process }
```

Replace RemoteComputer with the remote machine's name or IP address. Replace Get-Process with the command you want to execute.

The command output will be displayed on your local machine.

# One-to-Many Remoting

One-to-Many Remoting allows you to execute commands on multiple remote machines simultaneously. This can be particularly useful for managing a group of computers or performing bulk actions. You can achieve One-to-Many Remoting using the Invoke-Command cmdlet.

To perform One-to-Many Remoting, follow these steps:

Open PowerShell on your local machine.

Create a list of remote machines you want to connect to. You can store the list in an array or a text file:

# Array Example

$RemoteComputers = @('RemoteComputer1', 'RemoteComputer2', 'RemoteComputer3')

# Text File Example

$RemoteComputers = Get-Content -Path "C:\path\to\remote_computers.txt"

Use the Invoke-Command cmdlet with the -ComputerName parameter, passing the list of remote machines, and the command or scriptblock to execute:

Invoke-Command -ComputerName $RemoteComputers -ScriptBlock { Get-Service }

Replace Get-Service with the command you want to execute.

The command output from each remote machine will be displayed on your local machine. By understanding and implementing One-to-One and One-to-Many Remoting, you can efficiently manage remote systems, execute commands, and automate tasks across multiple machines in a Windows environment.

# Sessions and Persistent Connections

In PowerShell Remoting, sessions and persistent connections are essential concepts to manage remote machines effectively. Sessions, known as PSSessions, represent a persistent connection to a remote machine that allows you to execute multiple commands without having to re-establish the connection each time. This can be more efficient and help you manage multiple systems simultaneously.

Given below is a detailed explanation of PSSessions and persistent connections, along with illustrations of how to work with them:

## Creating a PSSession

To create a PSSession, use the New-PSSession cmdlet with the -ComputerName parameter followed by the remote machine's name or IP address:

```
$Session = New-PSSession -ComputerName RemoteComputer
```

Replace RemoteComputer with the remote machine's name or IP address. The newly created session is stored in the $Session variable.

## Executing Commands using a PSSession

Once you have created a PSSession, you can use the Invoke-Command cmdlet with the -Session parameter to execute commands on the remote machine:

```
Invoke-Command -Session $Session -ScriptBlock { Get-Process }
```

Replace Get-Process with the command you want to execute on the remote machine. You can execute multiple commands without having to re-establish the connection each time.

## Entering and Exiting Interactive PSSession

You can also enter an interactive session using a PSSession, allowing you to execute commands as if you were logged in directly to the remote machine. To enter an interactive session, use the Enter-PSSession cmdlet with the -Session parameter:

```
Enter-PSSession -Session $Session
```

To exit the interactive session, use the Exit-PSSession cmdlet:

```
Exit-PSSession
```

## Importing Remote Commands using a PSSession

You can import remote commands from a PSSession into your local session, making them available as if they were local commands. This is known as Implicit Remoting. To import remote commands, use the Import-PSSession cmdlet:

```
$ImportedSession = Import-PSSession -Session $Session -Module RemoteModule
```

Replace RemoteModule with the name of the remote module you want to import. The imported commands are stored in the $ImportedSession variable.

## Removing a PSSession

When you no longer need a PSSession, it's essential to remove it to free up resources. To remove a PSSession, use the Remove-PSSession cmdlet:

Remove-PSSession -Session $Session

This will close the connection and release the resources associated with the PSSession.

To summarize, understanding and working with PSSessions and persistent connections in PowerShell Remoting allows you to efficiently manage remote systems, execute multiple commands without re-establishing connections, and import remote commands into your local session. Using these techniques will help you streamline your remote administration and automation tasks.

# Remote Troubleshooting and Management

Remote troubleshooting and management are essential tasks for system administrators, especially when dealing with multiple machines in a network. PowerShell Remoting is a powerful tool that can help you perform these tasks efficiently. Given below is a detailed guide on using PowerShell Remoting for remote troubleshooting and management:

## Gathering System Information

To troubleshoot and manage remote systems, you first need to gather information about them. Use the Invoke-Command cmdlet to run commands that provide system information:

*Get system information using Get-ComputerInfo:*

Invoke-Command -ComputerName RemoteComputer -ScriptBlock { Get-ComputerInfo }

*List installed updates using Get-Hotfix:*

Invoke-Command -ComputerName RemoteComputer -ScriptBlock { Get-

Hotfix }

*Check disk space using Get-PSDrive:*

Invoke-Command -ComputerName RemoteComputer -ScriptBlock { Get-PSDrive -PSProvider FileSystem }

# Replace RemoteComputer with Remote Machine's Name

You can manage services on remote machines using the *-Service cmdlets with Invoke-Command:

*Get the status of a service:*

Invoke-Command -ComputerName RemoteComputer -ScriptBlock { Get-Service -Name ServiceName }

*Start a service:*

Invoke-Command -ComputerName RemoteComputer -ScriptBlock { Start-Service -Name ServiceName }

*Stop a service:*

Invoke-Command -ComputerName RemoteComputer -ScriptBlock { Stop-Service -Name ServiceName }

Replace RemoteComputer with the remote machine's name or IP address and ServiceName with the name of the service you want to manage.

# Managing Processes

You can manage processes on remote machines using the *-Process cmdlets with Invoke-Command:

*Get a list of running processes:*

Invoke-Command -ComputerName RemoteComputer -ScriptBlock { Get-Process }

*Terminate a process:*

Invoke-Command -ComputerName RemoteComputer -ScriptBlock { Stop-Process -Id ProcessId }

Replace RemoteComputer with the remote machine's name or IP address and ProcessId with the ID of the process you want to terminate.

## Managing Windows Features

You can manage Windows features on remote machines using the *-WindowsFeature cmdlets with Invoke-Command:

*List installed Windows features:*

Invoke-Command -ComputerName RemoteComputer -ScriptBlock { Get-WindowsFeature }

*Install a Windows feature:*

Invoke-Command -ComputerName RemoteComputer -ScriptBlock { Install-WindowsFeature -Name FeatureName }

*Uninstall a Windows feature:*

Invoke-Command -ComputerName RemoteComputer -ScriptBlock { Uninstall-WindowsFeature -Name FeatureName }

Replace RemoteComputer with the remote machine's name or IP address and FeatureName with the name of the Windows feature you want to manage.

## Executing Scripts on Remote Machines

You can execute scripts on remote machines to perform more complex troubleshooting and management tasks:

```
Invoke-Command -ComputerName RemoteComputer -FilePath
"C:\path\to\your_script.ps1"
```

Replace RemoteComputer with the remote machine's name or IP address and provide the path to your script.

By understanding and utilizing PowerShell Remoting for remote troubleshooting and management, you can efficiently

# Securing PowerShell Remoting

When securing PowerShell Remoting, it's important to consider several key aspects to ensure that the system is adequately protected. One of the first steps is to establish secure communication channels through the use of SSL encryption or HTTPS. Additionally, limiting remote access to trusted individuals or groups and configuring firewalls to only allow authorized traffic can help prevent unauthorized access. Furthermore, using strong authentication mechanisms such as multi-factor authentication and implementing logging and auditing features can aid in maintaining system integrity and identifying potential security breaches. Regularly updating and patching the system can also help to address any known vulnerabilities. By taking these steps, administrators can better secure PowerShell Remoting and reduce the risk of sensitive information being compromised.

## Configure WinRM Service

WinRM, short for Windows Remote Management, serves as the backbone of PowerShell Remoting. When it comes to using WinRM, one of the most important things to consider is security. To safeguard your system, it's essential to verify that the WinRM service is up and running, and that it's configured to start automatically. By taking these steps, you can help ensure that your system is well-protected against potential security threats that may target WinRM.

```
Set-Service -Name WinRM -StartupType Automatic
Start-Service -Name WinRM
```

# Use Secure Transports

When establishing remote connections, use HTTPS instead of HTTP to encrypt the communication. To enable HTTPS, you'll need an SSL certificate installed on the remote machine. You can generate a self-signed certificate or use a certificate issued by a trusted certificate authority (CA).

To create a new HTTPS listener with a specific certificate thumbprint, run:

New-Item -Path WSMan:\LocalHost\Listener -Transport HTTPS -Address * - CertificateThumbPrint 'YourCertificateThumbprint' -Force

Replace 'YourCertificateThumbprint' with the thumbprint of the certificate you want to use.

# Configure Firewall Rules

To safeguard your computer or network against unauthorized access, it is crucial to configure your firewall settings to only allow incoming connections from trusted sources. This can be achieved by creating specific firewall rules using either the in-built Windows Firewall or any third-party firewall software. By limiting access to only trusted networks or IP addresses, you can prevent malicious attacks, viruses, and other security threats from infiltrating your system. Regularly reviewing and updating your firewall settings is a critical component of maintaining the security of your computer or network..

# Use Strong Authentication Mechanisms

To ensure secure communication, PowerShell Remoting supports several authentication mechanisms, such as Kerberos, NTLM, and CredSSP. Among them, Kerberos is the default and recommended option for domain-joined computers, as it provides strong security and seamless authentication for domain users. However, in non-domain environments, you can use alternative mechanisms like CredSSP or certificate-based authentication, which provide flexibility and enable more granular control over authentication and authorization. It's essential to choose the appropriate authentication mechanism depending on the security requirements and environment configurations to ensure safe and efficient communication between PowerShell endpoints.

To enable CredSSP, run the following commands on the remote machine:

Enable-WSManCredSSP -Role Server

On the local machine, run:

```
Enable-WSManCredSSP -Role Client -DelegateComputer RemoteComputer
```

Replace 'RemoteComputer' with the remote machine's name or IP address.

## Restrict User Access

To enhance the security of remote machines, it is important to limit the number of users who have access to them. This can be achieved by adding only necessary users or groups to the local "Remote Management Users" group or implementing Just Enough Administration (JEA). JEA provides granular permissions that allow users to perform specific tasks without giving them full administrative access. By limiting access in this way, organizations can reduce the risk of unauthorized access and potential security breaches.

## Configure Execution Policy

PowerShell's Execution Policy is a critical security feature that helps protect the system from malicious scripts. By default, PowerShell restricts the execution of scripts to prevent unauthorized access to the system. Users can configure the Execution Policy to a more permissive level, but this can also increase the risk of running potentially harmful scripts. It is important to set the Execution Policy to a suitable level, such as RemoteSigned or AllSigned, to prevent the execution of unsigned or untrusted scripts and maintain a high level of security.

```
Set-ExecutionPolicy RemoteSigned
```

## Auditing and Logging

To effectively monitor PowerShell Remoting activities, it's crucial to enable auditing and logging. Windows Event Log or third-party solutions can be used to collect and analyze logs for any suspicious activities. This helps to identify any unauthorized access, changes or malicious activities and take necessary actions to prevent security breaches. Regular monitoring of logs is essential for maintaining the security and integrity of the system.

To enable module logging, add the following to the 'PowerShellScriptExecutionSettings' Group Policy setting:

```
<Configuration>
```

```
<LogPipelineExecutionDetails>true</LogPipelineExecutionDetails>
<ScriptBlockLogging>

<EnableScriptBlockInvocationLogging>true</EnableScriptBlockInvocationLogging>
  </ScriptBlockLogging>
</Configuration>
```

## Update PowerShell and Related Components

It is essential to keep PowerShell, WinRM, and their associated components up to date to ensure optimal security. Regularly updating these components ensures that you receive the latest security patches and enhancements, providing a robust defense against potential threats. By staying current with updates, you can avoid security vulnerabilities and keep your systems running smoothly.

By implementing these security practices, you can effectively secure PowerShell Remoting, protect your systems from unauthorized access, and maintain a robust security posture in your environment.

# CHAPTER 10: POWERSHELL DESIRED STATE CONFIGURATION (DSC)

# Introduction to DSC

PowerShell Desired State Configuration (DSC) is a powerful configuration management platform that enables administrators to automate the deployment, management, and maintenance of infrastructure resources in their computing environments. Developed by Microsoft, DSC is built on top of the PowerShell scripting language and leverages its extensive capabilities to help administrators manage the state of their systems more effectively.

DSC operates using a declarative syntax, which means that administrators only need to describe the desired state of their systems, rather than specifying the individual steps necessary to achieve that state. This simplifies the configuration process and reduces the risk of errors caused by manual intervention or complex scripts.

One of the core components of PowerShell DSC is the configuration script, which is essentially a PowerShell script with a specific structure. It contains a series of declarative statements that describe the desired state of the system. These statements, known as resources, define the various components to be configured, such as files, registry keys, services, or software packages. Another critical component of DSC is the Local Configuration Manager (LCM), which is responsible for interpreting and applying the configuration scripts on target nodes. The LCM regularly checks the system's current state against the desired state defined in the configuration script and takes appropriate actions to correct any discrepancies.

# DSC Benefits for SysAdmin

PowerShell administrators benefit from DSC in several ways:
- Standardization: By using DSC, administrators can enforce consistent configurations across their infrastructure, ensuring that all systems adhere to predefined standards. This reduces the risk of configuration drift and helps maintain a stable and predictable environment.
- Scalability: DSC enables administrators to manage large-scale environments with ease, as it can be used to configure multiple systems simultaneously. This saves time and effort compared to manually configuring each system individually.
- Version control and change tracking: DSC configuration scripts can be stored in version control systems, allowing administrators to track changes and roll back to previous configurations if necessary. This provides better visibility and control over the infrastructure's evolution.
- Simplified troubleshooting: Since DSC ensures that systems are configured consistently, troubleshooting becomes more straightforward. Administrators can quickly identify and resolve issues caused by configuration drift or inconsistencies.

- Integration with other automation tools: DSC can be integrated with popular automation and orchestration platforms, such as Chef, Puppet, and Ansible. This enables administrators to leverage existing workflows and tools, enhancing their overall automation capabilities.
- Cross-platform support: Although initially designed for Windows, DSC now supports Linux systems as well, allowing administrators to manage heterogeneous environments using a single configuration management platform.
- Continuous deployment and integration: DSC supports the principles of continuous deployment and integration, enabling administrators to automate the process of deploying and configuring applications and services in their environments. This accelerates the release cycle and improves the overall efficiency of the IT operations.
- Enhanced security: By automating the configuration process, DSC reduces the risk of human error and misconfigurations that can lead to security vulnerabilities. Administrators can also use DSC to enforce security policies and ensure that systems

# Writing and Applying DSC Configurations

Desired State Configuration (DSC) is a management platform in PowerShell that allows you to manage and configure your infrastructure in a standardized, automated, and idempotent (repeatable) manner. DSC allows you to define configurations in a declarative language and apply them to target nodes (such as servers or workstations).

# Writing DSC Configurations

To write a DSC configuration, you need to create a PowerShell script (.ps1) that uses the Configuration keyword followed by the name you want to give your configuration. Inside the configuration block, you define the target nodes, resources, and their desired states. Given below is a simple example:

```
Configuration MyDSCConfiguration {
   Node 'localhost' {
     File ExampleFile {
        DestinationPath = 'C:\Example\example.txt'
        Ensure = 'Present'
        Contents = 'Hello, DSC!'
     }
```

```
    }
}
```

In the above given sample program, we have a configuration named MyDSCConfiguration that targets the local host. The configuration ensures that there's a file named 'example.txt' in the 'C:\Example' folder with the content 'Hello, DSC!'.

# Applying DSC Configurations

To apply a DSC configuration, you need to follow these steps:

## *Generate a MOF file from your configuration*

After writing your DSC configuration, you need to generate a Managed Object Format (MOF) file that contains the metadata required to apply the configuration to the target node. To do this, simply call the configuration like a function:

## MyDSCConfiguration

This will generate a MOF file in the folder '.\MyDSCConfiguration\localhost.mof'.

## *Apply the MOF file to the target node*

Now that you have the MOF file, you need to apply it to the target node using the Start-DscConfiguration cmdlet:

## Start-DscConfiguration -Path .\MyDSCConfiguration -Wait -Verbose

This cmdlet will apply the configuration to the target node and provide verbose output so you can see the progress. The -Wait flag ensures that the cmdlet doesn't return until the configuration is complete.

That's a basic example of writing and applying a DSC configuration. Remember that DSC provides a lot more functionality and resources, allowing you to manage a wide range of configuration settings.

For more information, refer to the official documentation:
- DSC overview: https://docs.microsoft.com/en-us/powershell/scripting/dsc/overview/overview
- DSC resources: https://docs.microsoft.com/en-

# Creating Custom DSC Resources

Creating custom Desired State Configuration (DSC) resources involves three main steps:
- Design the resource: Identify the configuration settings you want to manage and determine the properties required to configure them.
- Implement the resource: Create a PowerShell script module that implements the Get, Set, and Test functions for your custom resource.
- Package the resource: Package your custom resource as a module and make it available to the DSC engine by placing it in the appropriate folder or registering it in a DSC pull server.

Given below is a practical illustration of creating a custom DSC resource:

## Design the Resource

Let us create a custom DSC resource to manage the state of a Windows service.

Our custom resource will have the following properties:
- Name: The name of the Windows service.
- State: The desired state of the service ('Running' or 'Stopped').

## Implement the Resource

Create a new folder named DSCResources and, within it, another folder named cWindowsService. Inside the cWindowsService folder, create a schema file named cWindowsService.schema.mof with the following content:

```
[ClassVersion("1.0.0"), FriendlyName("cWindowsService")]
class cWindowsService : OMI_BaseResource
{
   [Key, Description("The name of the Windows service.")] String Name;
   [Write, Description("The desired state of the service."),
ValueMap{"Running", "Stopped"}, Values{"Running", "Stopped"}] String
State;
};
```

Next, create a PowerShell script module named cWindowsService.psm1 in the cWindowsService folder with the following content:

```
using namespace System.Management.Automation
using namespace System.Management.Automation.Language

[CmdletBinding()]
param ()

function Get-TargetResource {
  [CmdletBinding()]
  [OutputType([System.Collections.Hashtable])]
  param (
    [parameter(Mandatory = $true)]
    [string]$Name,
    [ValidateSet("Running", "Stopped")]
    [string]$State
  )

  $service = Get-Service -Name $Name -ErrorAction SilentlyContinue
  $result = @{
    Name  = $Name
    State = $service.Status.ToString()
  }

  return $result
}

function Set-TargetResource {
  [CmdletBinding()]
  param (
    [parameter(Mandatory = $true)]
```

```
        [string]$Name,
        [ValidateSet("Running", "Stopped")]
        [string]$State
    )

    $service = Get-Service -Name $Name -ErrorAction SilentlyContinue
    if ($State -eq "Running") {
        if ($service.Status -ne "Running") {
            Start-Service -Name $Name
        }
    } elseif ($State -eq "Stopped") {
        if ($service.Status -ne "Stopped") {
            Stop-Service -Name $Name
        }
    }
}

function Test-TargetResource {
    [CmdletBinding()]
    [OutputType([System.Boolean])]
    param (
        [parameter(Mandatory = $true)]
        [string]$Name,
        [ValidateSet("Running", "Stopped")]
        [string]$State
    )

    $service = Get-Service -Name $Name -ErrorAction SilentlyContinue
    return ($service.Status.ToString() -eq $State)
}

Export-ModuleMember -Function *-TargetResource
```

This script module implements the Get, Set, and Test functions for our custom cWindowsService resource.

## Package the Resource

Zip the DSCResources folder and rename the zip file to DSCResources.zip. This zip file is now a module that contains our custom DSC resource. To make it available to the DSC engine, you can either place the DSCResources folder in the appropriate folder on the target node or register it in a DSC pull server.

For local use, copy the DSCResources folder to one of the following locations:

$env:ProgramFiles\WindowsPowerShell\Modules (for all users)
$env:USERPROFILE\Documents\WindowsPowerShell\Modules (for the current user)

Now, you can use the custom DSC resource cWindowsService in your DSC configurations:

```
Configuration CustomResourceExample {
  Import-DscResource -ModuleName DSCResources -Name
cWindowsService

  Node 'localhost' {
    cWindowsService MyService {
      Name  = 'MyServiceName'
      State = 'Running'
    }
  }
}


CustomResourceExample
Start-DscConfiguration -Path .\CustomResourceExample -Wait -Verbose
```

In the above given sample program, we import our custom resource using Import-

DscResource and use it in the DSC configuration. The configuration ensures that the service with the name 'MyServiceName' is in the 'Running' state on the local host.

# DSC Configuration Management and Reporting

Managing Desired State Configuration (DSC) and generating reports can be done using a few key cmdlets and techniques. We'll discuss how to monitor and report on DSC configurations using:

- Local Configuration Manager (LCM) logs.
- DSC reporting through a pull server.

## Local Configuration Manager (LCM) Logs

LCM is the engine that processes and enforces DSC configurations on target nodes. It generates logs that can help you monitor and troubleshoot DSC configurations. To access these logs, you can use the Get-WinEvent cmdlet:

Get-WinEvent -LogName 'Microsoft-Windows-DSC/Operational'

You can filter these logs based on a specific event ID or time range, for example:

Get-WinEvent -LogName 'Microsoft-Windows-DSC/Operational' -FilterXPath '*[System/EventID=4103]'

This command retrieves events with the ID 4103, which indicates successful resource configuration.

## DSC Reporting Through Pull Server

A pull server is a central location where target nodes pull configurations and custom resources. The pull server can also collect status reports from the target nodes. When you use a pull server, the reporting data is stored in a database, making it easier to manage and generate reports.

To configure reporting on a pull server, you need to:

Set up a pull server if you haven't already. Instructions can be found in the official documentation: https://docs.microsoft.com/en-us/powershell/scripting/dsc/pull-server/pullserversetup

Configure the target nodes to send reports to the pull server. This can be done by configuring LCM on each target node:

```
[DSCLocalConfigurationManager()]
Configuration LCMConfiguration {
  Node 'localhost' {
    Settings {
      RefreshMode         = 'Pull'
      ConfigurationID     = 'your-configuration-guid'
      RebootNodeIfNeeded   = $true
      ConfigurationMode    = 'ApplyAndAutoCorrect'
      ConfigurationModeFrequencyMins = 30
      RefreshFrequencyMins = 15
    }

    ConfigurationRepositoryWeb PullServer {
      ServerURL         = 'https://your-pull-server-
url:port/PSDSCPullServer.svc'
      RegistrationKey   = 'your-registration-key'
      ConfigurationNames = @('your-configuration-name')
    }

    ReportServerWeb PullServer {
      ServerURL       = 'https://your-pull-server-
url:port/PSDSCPullServer.svc'
      RegistrationKey = 'your-registration-key'
    }
  }
}
```

LCMConfiguration
Set-DscLocalConfigurationManager -Path .\LCMConfiguration

Query the status reports from the pull server. You can use the xDscDiagnostics module to retrieve the reports:

Install-Module xDscDiagnostics
Import-Module xDscDiagnostics
Get-xDscOperation -Newest 10 -PullServerEndpoint 'https://your-pull-server-url:port/PSDSCPullServer.svc'

This command retrieves the 10 newest status reports from the pull server.

With these techniques, you can monitor DSC configurations, troubleshoot issues, and generate reports to ensure that your infrastructure is in the desired state.

# CHAPTER 11: POWERSHELL AND SYSTEM CENTER CONFIGURATION MANAGER (SCCM)

# Understanding SCCM

PowerShell and System Center Configuration Manager (SCCM) can be used together to manage and automate various tasks related to configuration, deployment, and monitoring of devices and applications within an organization. SCCM, also known as ConfigMgr or MEMCM (Microsoft Endpoint Manager Configuration Manager), is a comprehensive management solution for Windows-based environments, providing centralized control over various aspects of IT infrastructure.

PowerShell is a powerful scripting language and automation framework that complements SCCM in several ways:

## Automation

By using PowerShell, you can automate repetitive or complex tasks in SCCM, such as creating and modifying collections, deploying applications, managing boundaries, or configuring client settings. This can save time, reduce human error, and improve overall efficiency.

## Integration

PowerShell can interact with SCCM through its PowerShell module, which includes cmdlets for managing SCCM components. The module allows you to perform various SCCM operations, such as querying or modifying site settings, managing deployments, and generating reports.

## Customization

PowerShell scripts can be used to extend SCCM functionality, such as creating custom actions or integrating with third-party tools and services. This can help tailor SCCM to the unique needs of your organization.

## Troubleshooting

PowerShell can be used to gather diagnostic information, query log files, or perform health checks on SCCM components. This can help identify and resolve issues faster, improving the stability and reliability of your environment.

# Procedure to Use SCCM with PowerShell

Here are some examples of how you can use PowerShell with SCCM:

# Load SCCM PowerShell Module

Before you can use PowerShell cmdlets for SCCM, you need to load the SCCM PowerShell module. You can do this by running the following command:

```
Import-Module (Join-Path $(Split-Path $env:SMS_ADMIN_UI_PATH) ConfigurationManager.psd1)
```

# Connect to SCCM Site

To connect to an SCCM site, use the Connect-CMSite cmdlet:

```
Connect-CMSite -ComputerName SCCMSiteServer -Credential (Get-Credential)
```

Replace SCCMSiteServer with the name of your SCCM site server.

# Query Device Collections

To query device collections, you can use the Get-CMDeviceCollection cmdlet:

```
Get-CMDeviceCollection
```

# Create New Device Collection

To create a new device collection, use the New-CMDeviceCollection cmdlet:

```
New-CMDeviceCollection -Name "New Device Collection" -LimitingCollectionName "All Systems" -RefreshType Periodic -RefreshSchedule (New-CMSchedule -Start "01/01/2023 00:00" -DayOfWeek Monday -RecurCount 1)
```

Replace the values as needed to match your desired configuration.

# Deploy Application

To deploy an application, use the Start-CMApplicationDeployment cmdlet:

```
Start-CMApplicationDeployment -CollectionName "Target Collection" -Name
"Application Name" -DeployAction Install -DeployPurpose Available -
UserNotification DisplaySoftwareCenterOnly -AvailableDateTime "01/01/2023
00:00"
```

Replace the values as needed to match your desired configuration.

By leveraging the power of PowerShell in conjunction with SCCM, you can efficiently manage, automate, and customize your organization's IT infrastructure, improving overall productivity and reducing the chances of human error.

# Deploying and Managing Applications

Managing and deploying applications using SCCM and PowerShell involves several steps, such as creating an application, distributing content, and deploying the application to a target collection. The following steps outline the process in detail:

## Create Application in SCCM

Before using PowerShell, you need to create an application in SCCM. Follow these general steps:
- In the SCCM console, navigate to "Software Library" > "Application Management" > "Applications."
- Right-click "Applications" and select "Create Application."
- Follow the wizard to specify the application's source files, detection method, deployment type, and other settings.

## Distribute the Application Content

After creating the application, distribute its content to Distribution Points (DPs) using PowerShell. The Start-CMContentDistribution cmdlet can be used for this purpose.

First, retrieve the application and distribution point information using Get-CMApplication and Get-CMDistributionPoint cmdlets:

```
$Application = Get-CMApplication -Name "Application Name"
$DistributionPoint = Get-CMDistributionPoint -SiteSystemServerName
"DPName"
```

Replace "Application Name" with the name of your application, and "DPName" with the name of your distribution point server.

Next, distribute the content:

Start-CMContentDistribution -ApplicationId $Application.CI_ID -DistributionPointGroupName $DistributionPoint.GroupName

# Deploy Application to Target Collection

To deploy the application to a target collection, use the Start-CMApplicationDeployment cmdlet. First, retrieve the target collection information using the Get-CMDeviceCollection cmdlet:

$TargetCollection = Get-CMDeviceCollection -Name "Target Collection Name"

Replace "Target Collection Name" with the name of the collection you want to deploy the application to.

Now, deploy the application:

Start-CMApplicationDeployment -CollectionId $TargetCollection.CollectionID -Name $Application.LocalizedDisplayName -DeployAction Install -DeployPurpose Available -UserNotification DisplaySoftwareCenterOnly -AvailableDateTime (Get-Date)

Adjust the parameters as needed. For example, you can change the -DeployPurpose to "Required" if you want to force the installation, or modify the -AvailableDateTime to schedule the deployment.

# Monitor the Deployment

To monitor the deployment status, use the Get-CMDeploymentStatus cmdlet. First, retrieve the deployment information using the Get-CMDeployment cmdlet:

$Deployment = Get-CMDeployment -CollectionName $TargetCollection.Name

-ApplicationName $Application.LocalizedDisplayName

Next, query the deployment status:

Get-CMDeploymentStatus -DeploymentID $Deployment.DeploymentID

This will display the deployment status for all devices in the target collection. You can filter the results or export them to a file for further analysis.

By following these steps, you can manage and deploy applications using SCCM and PowerShell effectively. This allows you to automate application deployments, monitor their status, and manage your organization's software efficiently.

# Managing Software Updates and Patches

Performing software updates and patches through SCCM and PowerShell involves several steps, such as synchronizing software updates, creating software update groups, deploying the updates, and monitoring the update deployment. The following steps outline the process in detail:

## Synchronize Software Updates

First, synchronize software updates in the SCCM console. This process downloads the latest update catalog from Microsoft Update or other configured update sources.

To synchronize software updates using PowerShell, you can use the Start-CMSoftwareUpdateSync cmdlet:

Start-CMSoftwareUpdateSync

## Create a Software Update Group

After synchronizing updates, create a Software Update Group to group relevant updates together for deployment. You can create a Software Update Group using the New-CMSoftwareUpdateGroup cmdlet:

$UpdateGroup = New-CMSoftwareUpdateGroup -Name "My Update Group"

# Add Updates to Software Update Group

Search and add the relevant updates to the Software Update Group using the Get-CMSoftwareUpdate and Add-CMSoftwareUpdateToGroup cmdlets. For example, you can search for updates based on criteria such as title, date released, and classification:

```
$Updates = Get-CMSoftwareUpdate -DateReleasedMin (Get-Date).AddMonths(-1) -UpdateClassification "Critical Updates", "Security Updates"

foreach ($Update in $Updates) {
    Add-CMSoftwareUpdateToGroup -SoftwareUpdateId $Update.CI_ID -SoftwareUpdateGroupId $UpdateGroup.CI_ID
}
```

This example adds all critical and security updates released within the last month to the Software Update Group.

# Deploy Software Update Group

To deploy the Software Update Group to a target collection, use the Start-CMSoftwareUpdateDeployment cmdlet. First, retrieve the target collection information using the Get-CMDeviceCollection cmdlet:

```
$TargetCollection = Get-CMDeviceCollection -Name "Target Collection Name"
```

Replace "Target Collection Name" with the name of the collection you want to deploy the updates to.

Next, deploy the Software Update Group:

```
Start-CMSoftwareUpdateDeployment -SoftwareUpdateGroupName $UpdateGroup.LocalizedDisplayName -CollectionName $TargetCollection.Name -DeploymentType Required -SendWakeupPacket $true -UseUtc $true -AvailableDateTime (Get-Date) -DeadlineDateTime (Get-
```

Date).AddDays(7)

Adjust the parameters as needed, such as modifying the -AvailableDateTime and -DeadlineDateTime to set the availability and installation deadline for the updates.

## Monitor the Deployment

To monitor the update deployment status, use the Get-CMSoftwareUpdateDeploymentStatus cmdlet:

```
$DeploymentStatus = Get-CMSoftwareUpdateDeploymentStatus -
CollectionName $TargetCollection.Name -SoftwareUpdateGroupName
$UpdateGroup.LocalizedDisplayName
```

This will retrieve the deployment status for all devices in the target collection. You can filter the results, generate reports, or export them to a file for further analysis.

# Operating System Deployment Automation

Operating System Deployment (OSD) Automation is the process of automating the installation and configuration of operating systems on devices. This can be achieved using SCCM and PowerShell, allowing you to deploy custom operating system images and automate the configuration of settings, applications, and drivers.

Performing OSD automation involves several steps, such as creating and customizing an operating system image, creating a task sequence, deploying the task sequence, and monitoring the deployment. The following steps outline the process in detail:

## Create and Customize an Operating System Image

Create and customize an operating system image that includes your desired configuration, settings, applications, and drivers. You can use the SCCM console to create an image or use third-party tools such as Microsoft Deployment Toolkit (MDT) or Windows Assessment and Deployment Kit (ADK).

## Create a Task Sequence

Create a task sequence that defines the steps needed to install and configure the operating system image. You can create a task sequence using the SCCM console or PowerShell. For example, to create a new task sequence, use the New-CMTaskSequence cmdlet:

$TaskSequence = New-CMTaskSequence -Name "My Task Sequence"

## Add Steps to Task Sequence

Add steps to the task sequence that perform various tasks, such as configuring settings, installing applications, and running scripts. You can add steps using the SCCM console or PowerShell. For example, to add a step that installs an application, use the Add-CMTaskSequenceStepInstallApplication cmdlet:

Add-CMTaskSequenceStepInstallApplication -TaskSequenceId
$TaskSequence.PackageID -ApplicationName "My Application" -
ContinueOnError $false

## Deploy the Task Sequence

Deploy the task sequence to a target collection of devices using the SCCM console or PowerShell. To deploy the task sequence using PowerShell, you can use the New-CMDeviceCollectionDeployment cmdlet:

$TargetCollection = Get-CMDeviceCollection -Name "Target Collection
Name"
New-CMDeviceCollectionDeployment -CollectionName
$TargetCollection.Name -TaskSequenceName
$TaskSequence.LocalizedDisplayName -Purpose Required -
SendWakeUpPacket $true -DeployAction Install -AvailableDateTime (Get-
Date) -DeadlineDateTime (Get-Date).AddDays(7)

Adjust the parameters as needed, such as modifying the -AvailableDateTime and -DeadlineDateTime to set the availability and installation deadline for the task sequence.

## Monitor the Deployment

To monitor the task sequence deployment status, use the SCCM console or PowerShell. To retrieve the deployment status using PowerShell, use the Get-CMDeviceTaskSequenceDeploymentStatus cmdlet:

$DeploymentStatus = Get-CMDeviceTaskSequenceDeploymentStatus -
CollectionName $TargetCollection.Name -TaskSequenceName
$TaskSequence.LocalizedDisplayName

This will retrieve the deployment status for all devices in the target collection. You can filter the results, generate reports, or export them to a file for further analysis.

By following these steps, you can automate the installation and configuration of operating systems using SCCM and PowerShell, improving overall efficiency and reducing the chances of human error.

# SCCM Reporting and Monitoring

SCCM Reporting and Monitoring involves tracking and analyzing the health and performance of SCCM components and operations. SCCM provides various built-in reports and monitoring tools that allow you to monitor and report on various aspects of your environment, such as hardware and software inventory, software updates compliance, and device compliance.

You can also use PowerShell to retrieve SCCM data and generate custom reports and dashboards tailored to your organization's needs.

Here are some steps to perform SCCM Reporting and Monitoring using PowerShell:

## Load SCCM PowerShell Module

Before you can use SCCM cmdlets, you need to load the SCCM PowerShell module. You can do this by running the following command:

Import-Module (Join-Path $(Split-Path $env:SMS_ADMIN_UI_PATH)
ConfigurationManager.psd1)

## Retrieve SCCM Data

To retrieve SCCM data using PowerShell, use the relevant cmdlets. For example, to retrieve hardware inventory data for a device, use the Get-CMDeviceInventory cmdlet:

$Device = Get-CMDevice -Name "Device Name"

```
$Inventory = Get-CMDeviceInventory -DeviceId $Device.DeviceID
```

This will retrieve the hardware inventory data for the specified device. You can modify the parameters to retrieve data for multiple devices or filter the data based on various criteria.

# Generate Reports

To generate reports, use PowerShell to process the retrieved data and format it into a report. You can use PowerShell's built-in formatting and output cmdlets, such as Format-Table, Format-List, or Export-Csv, to create reports.

For example, to generate a report that lists all software updates and their compliance status for a specific device collection, you can use the following commands:

```
$Updates = Get-CMDeviceCollection -Name "Device Collection Name" | Get-CMSoftwareUpdateComplianceSummary
$Updates | Select-Object Title, KB, BulletinID, ComplianceState | Format-Table -AutoSize
```

This will generate a report that lists the software updates, their KB and bulletin IDs, and their compliance status for the specified device collection.

# Schedule Reports

You can schedule PowerShell scripts to run periodically and generate reports automatically. You can use Windows Task Scheduler to schedule PowerShell scripts to run at specific times or intervals.

For example, to schedule the software updates compliance report to run every week, you can create a PowerShell script that generates the report and save it to a file, such as "Generate-UpdatesComplianceReport.ps1". Then, use the Task Scheduler to create a new task that runs the script every week.

By using SCCM and PowerShell together, you can monitor and report on various aspects of your environment, improving overall visibility and control. By automating reporting and monitoring, you can save time, reduce manual effort, and improve efficiency.

# CHAPTER 12: POWERSHELL SECURITY AND BEST PRACTICES

# Secure Coding Practices

## Need for Secure Coding Practices

In a world where cyber-attacks are becoming increasingly sophisticated, security has become a top priority for organizations. PowerShell, being a versatile and powerful language, is an attractive target for attackers. They exploit poorly written scripts or vulnerabilities to gain unauthorized access, steal sensitive information, or disrupt operations. Therefore, it is imperative to adopt secure coding practices when working with PowerShell.

## Key Secure Coding Practices in PowerShell

### Minimize the use of hardcoded credentials

One common mistake made by script developers is hardcoding credentials within the script. This can expose sensitive information to attackers, leading to unauthorized access. To avoid this, use secure credential storage mechanisms such as Windows Credential Manager or Azure Key Vault.

### Validate input data

PowerShell scripts often rely on user inputs, configuration files, or other external sources. It is essential to validate this input data for correctness, format, and consistency to prevent injection attacks and other security risks. Utilize PowerShell's built-in validation attributes and custom validation functions to ensure data integrity.

### Employ least privilege principle

Limit the permissions and access levels of your PowerShell scripts. Grant only the required privileges for a script to function effectively, and nothing more. This minimizes the potential damage caused by unauthorized access or privilege escalation.

### Use signed scripts and script execution policies

PowerShell's script execution policies help prevent the execution of unauthorized or potentially malicious scripts. Set the execution policy to "AllSigned" or "RemoteSigned" to ensure that only trusted and signed scripts are executed. Additionally, use digital certificates to sign your scripts, ensuring their authenticity and integrity.

### Implement error handling and logging

Proper error handling and logging are crucial for detecting and responding to potential security threats. Include error handling in your scripts by using try-catch-finally blocks to capture and manage exceptions. Implement comprehensive logging to record script activities, which can be invaluable in incident response and forensic analysis.

## Secure remote connections

PowerShell remoting enables administrators to manage systems remotely. However, it can also be exploited by attackers. Ensure that you use encrypted connections, such as SSL/TLS, and authenticate users with mechanisms like Kerberos or certificate-based authentication.

## Avoid exposing sensitive information in logs and outputs

Be cautious about revealing sensitive information in logs, console outputs, or other external sources. Mask or redact sensitive data before writing to logs or outputs, ensuring that only authorized users have access to this information.

## Keep scripts and modules up-to-date

Regularly update your PowerShell scripts and modules to address security vulnerabilities and improve their overall security posture. Additionally, stay informed about the latest security best practices and incorporate them into your scripting processes.

## Perform security testing and code reviews

Regularly test your PowerShell scripts for security vulnerabilities and perform code reviews to identify and remediate any potential issues. Leverage automated testing tools and incorporate peer reviews to ensure comprehensive coverage.

## Educate and train developers and users

A key component of secure coding practices is raising awareness among developers and users. Conduct regular training sessions, workshops, and seminars to educate them about the importance of security and the secure coding practices specific to PowerShell.

Incorporating secure coding practices in PowerShell is a necessity for organizations to maintain a robust and secure infrastructure. By adopting these practices, organizations can minimize the risk of security breaches, safeguard sensitive information, and ensure the overall stability of their systems. As cyber threats continue to evolve, it is crucial for developers and administrators to stay informed about the latest security best practices and proactively implement them in their PowerShell scripting processes.

Secure coding practices in PowerShell play a critical role in protecting an organization's assets and ensuring its smooth operation. By following the guidelines outlined in this section, IT professionals can develop secure, reliable, and efficient PowerShell scripts, ultimately contributing to the organization's overall security posture. By consistently prioritizing security and adopting these best practices, organizations can reduce their vulnerability to cyber threats and foster a culture of security awareness and vigilance.

# PowerShell Execution Policy

PowerShell Execution Policy is a security feature that determines the conditions under which PowerShell loads configuration files and runs scripts. It helps to control the execution of scripts, thus mitigating the risk of running malicious or unauthorized scripts.

There are several predefined execution policies available:
- Restricted (Default): Does not allow any scripts to run, only permits individual commands.
- AllSigned: Only runs scripts that are signed by a trusted publisher.
- RemoteSigned: Runs locally-created scripts without requiring a signature, but scripts downloaded from the internet or received via email must be signed by a trusted publisher.
- Unrestricted: Allows all scripts to run, regardless of their origin or whether they are signed.
- Bypass: Disables the execution policy completely, offering no protection from potentially harmful scripts.
- Undefined: No execution policy is set, and the system defaults to the "Restricted" policy.

## Editing PowerShell Execution Policy

To change the PowerShell Execution Policy, you can use the Set-ExecutionPolicy cmdlet. You'll need to run PowerShell as an administrator to modify the policy.

Given below is how to change the execution policy:
- Open PowerShell with administrative privileges by searching for "PowerShell" in the Start menu, right-clicking on "Windows PowerShell", and selecting "Run as administrator".
- Check the current execution policy by running the following command: Get-ExecutionPolicy
- Change the execution policy by running the Set-ExecutionPolicy cmdlet followed by the desired policy, for example: Set-ExecutionPolicy RemoteSigned. You will be prompted to confirm the change.
- Verify that the policy has been updated by running Get-ExecutionPolicy again.

# Sample Program to Edit Execution Policy

Given below is a sample PowerShell script, "ChangeExecutionPolicy.ps1", that modifies the execution policy to "RemoteSigned":

```
# ChangeExecutionPolicy.ps1
$NewPolicy = "RemoteSigned"
$currentPolicy = Get-ExecutionPolicy

if ($currentPolicy -ne $NewPolicy) {
    Write-Output "Changing execution policy from $currentPolicy to $NewPolicy"
    Set-ExecutionPolicy $NewPolicy -Force
} else {
    Write-Output "Execution policy is already set to $NewPolicy"
}
```

To run this script, you will need to have administrative privileges in PowerShell, as modifying the execution policy requires administrator access. Follow these steps to run the script:

- Open PowerShell with administrative privileges by searching for "PowerShell" in the Start menu, right-clicking on "Windows PowerShell", and selecting "Run as administrator".
- Navigate to the directory containing the "ChangeExecutionPolicy.ps1" script using the cd command, for example: cd C:\path\to\your\
- Run the script with the following command: .\ChangeExecutionPolicy.ps1
- The script will display the current execution policy and change it to "RemoteSigned" if it's not already set to that. If you want to set a different execution policy, replace the value of the $NewPolicy variable with the desired policy, such as "AllSigned" or "Unrestricted".

# Bypassing PowerShell Execution Policy

Bypassing the PowerShell Execution Policy is not recommended, as it can expose your system to potential security risks. However, for educational purposes, here are a few ways to bypass the execution policy:

- Run a script with the "Bypass" policy for a single session: PowerShell.exe -ExecutionPolicy Bypass -File "path\to\your\script.ps1"

- Run a script as an argument to bypass policy restrictions: PowerShell.exe -Command "& { . 'path\to\your\script.ps1' }"
- Run a script by loading its content as a script block and invoking it: PowerShell.exe -Command "& { [ScriptBlock]::Create((Get-Content -Path 'path\to\your\script.ps1' -Raw)).Invoke() }"

Bypassing the execution policy can compromise the security of your system. Always exercise caution when working with PowerShell scripts and ensure you understand the implications of bypassing security features.

# Sample Program to Bypass Execution Policy

Given below is a sample PowerShell script, "SampleScript.ps1", that simply outputs "Hello, World!":

Write-Output "Hello, World!"

To execute this script, you would typically need to modify the execution policy to allow script execution. However, I'll demonstrate how to run this script without changing the policy permanently by using the bypass technique.

Run the script with the "Bypass" policy for a single session:

PowerShell.exe -ExecutionPolicy Bypass -File "C:\path\to\your\SampleScript.ps1"

Run the script as an argument to bypass policy restrictions:

PowerShell.exe -Command "& { . 'C:\path\to\your\SampleScript.ps1' }"

Run the script by loading its content as a script block and invoking it:

PowerShell.exe -Command "& { [ScriptBlock]::Create((Get-Content -Path 'C:\path\to\your\SampleScript.ps1' -Raw)).Invoke() }"

Remember to replace "C:\path\to\your" with the actual path to the directory where your "SampleScript.ps1" script is located.

# Constrained Language Mode

## Overview

Constrained Language Mode is a feature in PowerShell that restricts the language capabilities for increased security. It is designed to mitigate potential risks and exploits, such as PowerShell-based attacks, by limiting the availability of certain language elements that could be misused.

When Constrained Language Mode is enabled, several restrictions are applied, such as:
- Access to .NET types and methods is limited to a pre-approved set of types and methods considered safe.
- Scripters can only use basic language elements like variables, loops, and functions, while advanced language features like Add-Type, New-Object, and Invoke-Expression are blocked.
- Direct interaction with Windows API functions is restricted.

Constrained Language Mode is typically enforced using Windows Defender Application Control (WDAC) or AppLocker policies and is often applied in highly secure environments.

## Enable and Disable Constrained Language Mode

Enabling or disabling Constrained Language Mode is done through the use of WDAC, AppLocker, or Device Guard policies. For instance, you can create an AppLocker policy to enforce Constrained Language Mode:
- Open the Group Policy Management Editor (gpedit.msc).
- Navigate to "Computer Configuration" > "Policies" > "Windows Settings" > "Security Settings" > "Application Control Policies" > "AppLocker".
- Right-click "AppLocker" and choose "Properties".
- In the "PowerShell" tab, select "Enforce rules" to enable Constrained Language Mode or "Not configured" to disable it.
- Click "OK" to save the changes.

## Bypass Constrained Language Mode

To bypass Constrained Language Mode, you can either disable it using the same method mentioned above or execute scripts using an account that has permission to run scripts in Full Language Mode. This is often granted to administrators, who can run scripts using an elevated PowerShell session (i.e., "Run as administrator").

## Sample Program to Bypass Constrained Language Mode

Given below is a sample PowerShell script, "SampleScriptConstrained.ps1", that uses a blocked cmdlet (New-Object) in Constrained Language Mode:

```
# SampleScriptConstrained.ps1
try {
    $process = New-Object System.Diagnostics.Process
    $process.StartInfo.FileName = "notepad.exe"
    $process.Start()
    Write-Output "Notepad started successfully."
} catch {
    Write-Output "Error: Unable to start Notepad. This might be due to
Constrained Language Mode restrictions."
}
```

To bypass Constrained Language Mode and run this script, follow these steps:
- Open PowerShell with administrative privileges by searching for "PowerShell" in the Start menu, right-clicking on "Windows PowerShell", and selecting "Run as administrator".
- Navigate to the directory containing the "SampleScriptConstrained.ps1" script using the cd command, for example: cd C:\path\to\your\
- Run the script with the following command: .\SampleScriptConstrained.ps1

# Implementing Just Enough Administration (JEA)

Just Enough Administration (JEA) is a security feature in PowerShell that enables role-based access control (RBAC) for remote server administration. It allows organizations to grant specific administrative privileges to users without giving them full administrative rights. JEA ensures that users have access to just the necessary commands and resources required to perform their job, thereby reducing the risk of unauthorized access, privilege escalation, or accidental configuration changes.

JEA works by defining roles with specific access levels and mapping users to those roles. It leverages PowerShell session configurations (also known as "endpoints") to create restricted environments where users can execute a limited set of commands based on their

147

assigned roles.

To implement JEA, you will need to follow these steps:

# Install JEA PowerShell Module

On Windows Server 2016 and later, JEA is included by default. For earlier versions, you will need to install the JEA module using the following command:

Install-Module -Name JustEnoughAdministration -Force

# Define a Role Capability File

A Role Capability file (.psrc) is used to define the commands, cmdlets, functions, and external scripts that a specific role can use. Create a Role Capability file using the New-PSRoleCapabilityFile cmdlet:

New-PSRoleCapabilityFile -Path "C:\JEA\RoleCapabilities\HelpDesk.psrc"

Edit the "HelpDesk.psrc" file to define the allowed commands and resources for the HelpDesk role. For example:

```
@{
    GUID = 'Unique-GUID'
    ModulesToImport = 'ActiveDirectory'
    VisibleCmdlets = 'Get-ADUser', 'Get-ADComputer', 'Reset-
ADServiceAccountPassword', 'Unlock-ADAccount'
    VisibleExternalCommands = 'C:\Windows\System32\ping.exe'
}
```

Replace 'Unique-GUID' with a GUID that you can generate using the New-Guid cmdlet in PowerShell.

# Create a Session Configuration File

A Session Configuration file (.pssc) defines the JEA endpoint, including the virtual account to use, transcript settings, and the Role Capability files associated with the endpoint. Create a Session Configuration file using the New-PSSessionConfigurationFile cmdlet:

```
New-PSSessionConfigurationFile -Path
"C:\JEA\SessionConfigurations\HelpDesk.pssc" -SessionType
RestrictedRemoteServer -RunAsVirtualAccount -RoleDefinitions @{
    'CONTOSO\HelpDesk' = @{
        'RoleCapabilities' = 'HelpDesk'
    }
}
```

This example creates a JEA endpoint for the HelpDesk role, specifying that the commands will run as a virtual account and limiting access to members of the "CONTOSO\HelpDesk" group.

## Register the JEA Endpoint

Register the JEA endpoint using the Register-PSSessionConfiguration cmdlet:

```
Register-PSSessionConfiguration -Name "HelpDesk" -Path
"C:\JEA\SessionConfigurations\HelpDesk.pssc" -Force
```

## Test the JEA Endpoint

To test the JEA endpoint, connect to it using the Enter-PSSession cmdlet:

```
Enter-PSSession -ComputerName "ServerName" -ConfigurationName
"HelpDesk" -Credential (Get-Credential)
```

Replace "ServerName" with the name of the server where the JEA endpoint is registered. You will be prompted for credentials; enter the username and password for a user who is a member of the "CONTOSO\HelpDesk" group.

Once connected, you can execute the commands and functions defined in the Role Capability file for the HelpDesk role. You will not have access to any other PowerShell commands or functions outside of the ones explicitly defined in the Role Capability file.

To exit the JEA session, use the Exit-PSSession cmdlet.

JEA provides a powerful and flexible way to manage remote server administration, allowing organizations to grant specific privileges to users on a need-to-know basis. By defining Role Capability files and Session Configuration files, you can create custom endpoints with specific permissions and control what users can do on your servers.

# Auditing and Logging PowerShell Activities

PowerShell is a powerful scripting language that allows IT administrators and developers to automate tasks and manage system configurations. However, because PowerShell can execute commands that can potentially modify system settings and run scripts that may contain malicious code, it is important to implement auditing and logging practices to monitor and record PowerShell activities. Auditing and logging PowerShell activities provide critical insights into the actions performed by users, the scripts executed, and the impact on system configurations. In this section, we will discuss the necessity of auditing and logging PowerShell activities and how to implement it effectively.

## Necessity of Auditing and Logging PowerShell Activities

### Compliance Requirements

Many organizations are subject to compliance regulations, such as HIPAA, PCI-DSS, or SOX, which require them to maintain audit trails of activities that can impact system configurations or sensitive data. PowerShell activities fall into this category and must be audited and logged to comply with these regulations.

### Security

PowerShell is a popular tool for cyber attackers, who use it to execute malicious code and compromise systems. By monitoring and logging PowerShell activities, IT administrators can detect suspicious activity and identify potential security threats.

### Troubleshooting

PowerShell can be a powerful troubleshooting tool, but incorrect scripts or misconfigured commands can cause system issues. By logging PowerShell activities, IT administrators can identify the cause of the problem and take corrective action.

### Governance

Auditing and logging PowerShell activities help organizations maintain governance and control over their systems. By tracking who executed which command or script, IT administrators can ensure that policies and procedures are followed.

## Historical Analysis

PowerShell logs provide a historical record of system changes, making it easier to investigate issues, identify patterns, and perform root cause analysis.

# Implementing Auditing and Logging PowerShell Activities

To implement auditing and logging PowerShell activities, organizations can follow these best practices:

## Enable PowerShell logging

PowerShell logging can be enabled through Group Policy, PowerShell, or by modifying the registry. PowerShell logs can capture detailed information about PowerShell activities, including the executed scripts, commands, and their parameters. Organizations should ensure that the logs are stored securely and that log data is protected against tampering or deletion.

## Use script block logging

Script block logging captures detailed information about the script blocks that are executed, including the input, output, and errors generated. Script block logging is particularly useful for identifying the root cause of issues and detecting malicious activity.

## Implement log monitoring

Organizations should implement log monitoring tools to analyze PowerShell logs in real-time and detect potential security threats or unauthorized access. Log monitoring tools can generate alerts or trigger automated actions based on predefined rules, such as suspicious activity or unauthorized access attempts.

## Define auditing policies

Auditing policies should be defined based on the organization's compliance requirements and security policies. Auditing policies should specify which activities should be audited, who should be audited, and how long the audit logs should be retained.

## Use role-based access control

Role-based access control (RBAC) can limit the commands and scripts that users can execute, based on their assigned roles. RBAC can help prevent unauthorized access or execution of malicious code and ensure that users only have access to the necessary commands to perform their jobs.

To sum it up, auditing and logging PowerShell activities are critical for organizations to ensure compliance, maintain security, troubleshoot issues, and govern their systems. By implementing best practices, organizations can capture and analyze detailed information about PowerShell activities and detect potential security threats or unauthorized access. PowerShell logs provide valuable insights into system changes and can help organizations investigate issues, identify patterns, and perform root cause analysis.

# Sample program to enable powershell logging

Let us learn a sample program to enable PowerShell logging using Group Policy:
- Open the Group Policy Management Editor (gpedit.msc).
- Navigate to "Computer Configuration" > "Administrative Templates" > "Windows Components" > "Windows PowerShell".
- Double-click "Turn on PowerShell Script Block Logging".
- Select "Enabled".
- In the "Log script block invocation start/stop events" dropdown, select "Enabled".
- In the "Log non-script block invocation events" dropdown, select "Enabled".
- In the "Maximum size of the log file" dropdown, select "Enabled" and set the maximum size for the log file.
- Click "Apply" and "OK" to save the changes.

You can also enable PowerShell logging using the PowerShell console with the following commands:

```
Set-ItemProperty                                                    -Path
"HKLM:\Software\Policies\Microsoft\Windows\PowerShell\ScriptBlockLoggi
ng" -Name "EnableScriptBlockLogging" -Value 1
Set-ItemProperty                                                    -Path
"HKLM:\Software\Policies\Microsoft\Windows\PowerShell\ScriptBlockLoggi
ng" -Name "EnableInvocationLogging" -Value 1
Set-ItemProperty                                                    -Path
"HKLM:\Software\Policies\Microsoft\Windows\PowerShell\ScriptBlockLoggi
ng" -Name "LogPath" -Value "C:\Logs\PowerShell.log"
```

These commands enable script block and invocation logging and specify the log path where the logs will be stored. Replace "C:\Logs\PowerShell.log" with the desired log path.

Please note that enabling PowerShell logging can generate a significant amount of log data, which can affect system performance and require additional storage. It's important to configure logging settings carefully and regularly monitor the logs to ensure that they are being generated correctly and are capturing the desired information.

## Sample Program to Use Script Block Logging

Given below is a sample PowerShell script to enable and use script block logging:

```
# Enable Script Block Logging
Set-ItemProperty -Path "HKLM:\Software\Policies\Microsoft\Windows\PowerShell\ScriptBlockLoggi
ng" -Name "EnableScriptBlockLogging" -Value 1
Set-ItemProperty -Path "HKLM:\Software\Policies\Microsoft\Windows\PowerShell\ScriptBlockLoggi
ng" -Name "LogPath" -Value "C:\Logs\PowerShell.log"

# Enable Verbose Output and Script Block Logging
$VerbosePreference = "Continue"
$LogCommandHealthEvent = $true
$LogCommandLifecycleEvent = $true
$LogCommandPipelineExecutionDetail = $true

# Define a sample script block
$scriptBlock = {
    param($name)
    Write-Verbose "Hello, $name!"
}

# Invoke the script block and log the results
$scriptBlock.Invoke("John")

# View the logs
Get-Content -Path "C:\Logs\PowerShell.log"
```

This script enables script block logging by setting the necessary registry values, enables verbose output and script block logging, defines a sample script block that accepts a parameter, invokes the script block with the "Invoke" method, and logs the results to a log file specified by the "LogPath" registry value. Finally, the script reads the log file using the "Get-Content" cmdlet and outputs the log data to the console.

When this script is executed, it will create a log file in the specified directory ("C:\Logs\PowerShell.log") and log the details of the script block execution, including the input, output, and errors generated. The log data can be analyzed and monitored to detect potential security threats or unauthorized access.

Please note that script block logging can generate a significant amount of log data, which can affect system performance and require additional storage. It's important to configure logging settings carefully and regularly monitor the logs to ensure that they are being generated correctly and are capturing the desired information.

# CHAPTER 13: ADVANCED POWERSHELL TECHNIQUES

Advanced PowerShell techniques enable IT professionals and developers to perform complex tasks efficiently and with greater control. In this summary, we will explore five essential advanced techniques in PowerShell: Regular Expressions and Text Manipulation, Working with XML and JSON Data, Multithreading and Parallel Processing, Creating Custom Cmdlets and Modules, and Using .NET Framework and Assemblies in PowerShell.

## Regular Expressions and Text Manipulation

PowerShell, like other scripting languages, offers powerful tools for text manipulation using regular expressions. These expressions are patterns that describe character combinations in text and allow you to search, replace, and validate strings. PowerShell's -match and -replace operators enable you to work with regular expressions directly. The Select-String cmdlet can also search for patterns in text files, while the [regex] class offers more advanced methods for working with regular expressions, such as Matches(), Split(), and Replace().

## Working with XML and JSON Data

PowerShell can manipulate XML and JSON data formats natively, allowing you to work with structured data easily. For XML, you can create and parse documents using the [xml] type accelerator and interact with elements and attributes using familiar dot notation. Cmdlets like Import-Clixml, Export-Clixml, Select-Xml, and ConvertTo-Xml offer additional functionality for working with XML data.

For JSON, PowerShell provides the ConvertFrom-Json and ConvertTo-Json cmdlets to convert between JSON strings and PowerShell objects. Additionally, you can use the -Depth parameter to control the level of object conversion, and the -Compress and -Expand switches to control the output formatting.

## Multithreading and Parallel Processing

PowerShell offers several techniques to perform tasks concurrently, improving performance and responsiveness. The ForEach-Object -Parallel cmdlet allows you to run script blocks in parallel for each item in a collection, with the -ThrottleLimit parameter controlling the maximum number of parallel threads.
The Start-Job and Receive-Job cmdlets enable you to execute script blocks as background jobs, while Wait-Job can synchronize job completion. PowerShell workflows, although deprecated in PowerShell 7, offer another option for parallelism using the parallel keyword.

Finally, you can use the .NET System.Threading.Tasks.Parallel class and the System.Threading.Tasks.Task class to achieve more fine-grained control over multithreading and parallel processing in your scripts.

## Creating Custom Cmdlets and Modules

Custom cmdlets are specialized .NET classes that encapsulate specific functionality and can be used as regular PowerShell commands. To create a custom cmdlet, you need to create a .NET class that inherits from the Cmdlet or PSCmdlet base classes and implement the required methods, such as BeginProcessing(), ProcessRecord(), and EndProcessing(). Modules are collections of cmdlets, functions, aliases, and other resources that can be imported and shared. To create a module, you can write a PowerShell script (.psm1) or a .NET binary module (.dll). Place your module in one of the paths defined in $env:PSModulePath and use Import-Module to load it into your session.

## Using .NET Framework and Assemblies in PowerShell

PowerShell is built on the .NET framework, which means you can access .NET classes, methods, and properties directly in your scripts. You can create instances of .NET classes using the New-Object cmdlet or the [TypeName]::new() syntax. To access static members, use the [TypeName]::MemberName notation.

# Regular Expressions and Text Manipulation

You can use regular expressions and operators to perform various text manipulation tasks such as searching, replacing, splitting, and matching strings. Given below is a brief overview of how to use the -match, -replace, Matches(), Split(), and Replace() methods:

## -match Operator

The -match operator compares a string against a regular expression pattern and returns True if the pattern is found or False otherwise. The matches are stored in the automatic variable $matches.

Example:

```
$text = "PowerShell is a great scripting language."
$pattern = "\b\w{5}\b"
$result = $text -match $pattern
if ($result) {
   Write-Host "Match found: $($matches[0])"
} else {
   Write-Host "No match found"
}
```

# -replace Operator

The -replace operator allows you to replace occurrences of a pattern in a string with a specified replacement string.

Example:

```
$text = "PowerShell is a great scripting language."
$pattern = "\b\w{5}\b"
$replacement = "*****"
$newText = $text -replace $pattern, $replacement
Write-Host $newText
```

# Matches() Method

The [regex]::Matches() method returns a collection of all matches found in a string for a given regular expression pattern.

Example:

```
$text = "PowerShell is a great scripting language."
$pattern = "\b\w{5}\b"
$matches = [regex]::Matches($text, $pattern)
$matches | ForEach-Object { Write-Host $_.Value }
```

# Split() Method

The [regex]::Split() method allows you to split a string based on a regular expression pattern.

Example:

```
$text = "Name: John Doe, Age: 30, Location: New York"
$pattern = ",\s"
$splitText = [regex]::Split($text, $pattern)
$splitText | ForEach-Object { Write-Host $_ }
```

## Replace() Method

The [regex]::Replace() method is similar to the -replace operator, but it provides more advanced functionality. You can pass a script block or a MatchEvaluator delegate to perform complex replacement logic.

Example:

```
$text = "PowerShell is a great scripting language."
$pattern = "\b\w{5}\b"
$replacement = { param($match) return "*" * $match.Value.Length }
$newText = [regex]::Replace($text, $pattern, $replacement)
Write-Host $newText
```

These examples demonstrate basic usage of regular expressions and associated operators in PowerShell. You can build upon these examples and use more complex regular expressions to perform advanced text manipulation tasks.

# Working with XML and JSON Data

In PowerShell, Import-Clixml, Export-Clixml, Select-Xml, and ConvertTo-Xml cmdlets are primarily designed for working with XML data. For JSON data, you can use ConvertFrom-Json and ConvertTo-Json cmdlets. Given below is a brief overview and examples of how to use these cmdlets:

## Import-Clixml

Import-Clixml reads XML data from a file and converts it back to a PowerShell object.

Example:

```
# Save a sample object to an XML file
$sampleObject = @{
    Name = "John Doe"
    Age = 30
}
$sampleObject | Export-Clixml -Path "sampleObject.xml"
```

```
# Import the XML file back into a PowerShell object
$importedObject = Import-Clixml -Path "sampleObject.xml"
$importedObject
```

# Export-Clixml

Export-Clixml serializes a PowerShell object and saves it as an XML file.

Example:

```
$sampleObject = @{
    Name = "John Doe"
    Age = 30
}
$sampleObject | Export-Clixml -Path "sampleObject.xml"
```

# Select-Xml

Select-Xml searches for a specified XPath expression in XML content and returns the matching nodes.

Example:

```
[xml]$xmlContent = @"
<people>
  <person>
    <name>John Doe</name>
    <age>30</age>
  </person>
  <person>
    <name>Jane Doe</name>
    <age>28</age>
  </person>
</people>
```

"@

```
$xpath = "//person[name='John Doe']"
$selectedNode = Select-Xml -Xml $xmlContent -XPath $xpath
$selectedNode.Node.InnerXml
```

# ConvertTo-Xml

ConvertTo-Xml converts a PowerShell object into an XML-formatted string.

Example:

```
$sampleObject = @{
    Name = "John Doe"
    Age = 30
}
$xmlObject = $sampleObject | ConvertTo-Xml
$xmlObject.OuterXml
```

# ConvertFrom-Json

ConvertFrom-Json converts a JSON string to a PowerShell object.

Example:

```
$jsonString = '{"Name": "John Doe", "Age": 30}'
$convertedObject = ConvertFrom-Json -InputObject $jsonString
$convertedObject
```

# ConvertTo-Json

ConvertTo-Json converts a PowerShell object to a JSON string.

Example:

```
$sampleObject = @{
```

```
    Name = "John Doe"
    Age = 30
}
$jsonString = $sampleObject | ConvertTo-Json
$jsonString
```

These examples demonstrate the basic usage of PowerShell cmdlets for working with XML and JSON data. You can use these cmdlets in combination with other PowerShell features to manipulate, process, and transform structured data in your scripts.

# Multithreading and Parallel Processing

In PowerShell, you can use ForEach-Object with the -Parallel script block and the -ThrottleLimit parameter to perform multithreading and parallel processing. The -Parallel switch runs the script block concurrently for each item in a collection, while the -ThrottleLimit parameter controls the maximum number of concurrent threads.

Given below is a brief overview and examples of how to use ForEach-Object with -Parallel and -ThrottleLimit:

## ForEach-Object -Parallel

ForEach-Object with the -Parallel switch allows you to run a script block concurrently for each item in a collection.

Example:

```
$items = 1..10
$scriptBlock = {
    param($item)
    Start-Sleep -Seconds (Get-Random -Minimum 1 -Maximum 5)
    Write-Output "Processed item $item"
}
$items | ForEach-Object -Parallel $scriptBlock
```

# -ThrottleLimit

The -ThrottleLimit parameter controls the maximum number of concurrent threads when using ForEach-Object -Parallel.

Example:

```
$items = 1..10
$scriptBlock = {
    param($item)
    Start-Sleep -Seconds (Get-Random -Minimum 1 -Maximum 5)
    Write-Output "Processed item $item"
}
$items | ForEach-Object -Parallel $scriptBlock -ThrottleLimit 5
```

In the above given sample program, the script processes the items concurrently with a maximum of 5 parallel threads. Adjust the -ThrottleLimit value according to your system resources and the nature of the task for optimal performance.

Remember that when using parallel processing, the order of output may not be the same as the input order due to the concurrent execution of tasks. To maintain the order of output, you can use the Foreach-Object -Parallel -AsJob switch and the Receive-Job -Wait -AutoRemoveJob cmdlet.

Example:

```
$items = 1..10
$scriptBlock = {
    param($item)
    Start-Sleep -Seconds (Get-Random -Minimum 1 -Maximum 5)
    Write-Output "Processed item $item"
}
$job = $items | ForEach-Object -Parallel $scriptBlock -ThrottleLimit 5 -AsJob
$orderedOutput = Receive-Job -Job $job -Wait -AutoRemoveJob
$orderedOutput
```

These examples demonstrate the basic usage of ForEach-Object with -Parallel and -ThrottleLimit for multithreading and parallel processing in PowerShell. Use these techniques to improve the performance and responsiveness of your scripts when processing large collections or executing time-consuming tasks.

# Creating Custom Cmdlets and Modules

In PowerShell, you can create custom cmdlets and modules to streamline tasks and improve productivity. I'll give you a step-by-step guide to create a custom cmdlet and then bundle it into a module.

- Create a custom cmdlet using PowerShell script:

First, create a PowerShell script file (.ps1) that contains a function representing your custom cmdlet. The naming convention for cmdlets is Verb-Noun, such as Get-Information.

Example: Create a file called "Get-HelloWorld.ps1" with the following content:

```
function Get-HelloWorld {
    [CmdletBinding()]
    param (
        [Parameter(Mandatory=$false)]
        [string]$Name = "World"
    )

    Write-Output "Hello, $Name!"
}
```

This cmdlet takes an optional parameter Name and outputs "Hello, [Name]!".

- Test your custom cmdlet:

Before bundling it into a module, test the cmdlet by dot-sourcing the script file in a PowerShell session:

. .\Get-HelloWorld.ps1

- Now you can call your custom cmdlet:

Get-HelloWorld -Name "John"

- Create a PowerShell module:

To create a module, you'll need to create a folder with the same name as your module and place a .psm1 file inside it with the same name as the module.

Example: Create a folder called "MyCustomModule" and a file inside it called "MyCustomModule.psm1". Then, move your "Get-HelloWorld.ps1" file into this folder.

- Export functions as cmdlets in the module:

In the "MyCustomModule.psm1" file, you need to import the custom cmdlet script and export the function as a cmdlet. Modify the "MyCustomModule.psm1" file to include:

```
# Import custom cmdlet script
. .\Get-HelloWorld.ps1
```

```
# Export the function as a cmdlet
Export-ModuleMember -Function Get-HelloWorld
```

- Create a module manifest:

A module manifest (.psd1) file contains metadata about the module, such as author, version, and exported cmdlets. In the "MyCustomModule" folder, run the following command to create a manifest:

```
New-ModuleManifest -Path .\MyCustomModule.psd1 -RootModule
.\MyCustomModule.psm1
```

- Modify the module manifest:

Open the "MyCustomModule.psd1" file and update the metadata as needed. Most importantly, ensure that the FunctionsToExport field lists the cmdlets you want to export:

FunctionsToExport = @('Get-HelloWorld')

- Import and use your custom module:

Place the "MyCustomModule" folder in one of the directories listed in the $env:PSModulePath environment variable, or add your module path to the $env:PSModulePath.

- Now you can import your custom module in a PowerShell session:

Import-Module MyCustomModule

- And use the custom cmdlet:

Get-HelloWorld -Name "John"

That's it! You've created a custom cmdlet, bundled it into a module, and imported it for use. You can add more custom cmdlets to your module by following the same process.

# Using .NET Framework and Assemblies

PowerShell is built on top of the .NET Framework, which allows you to interact with .NET classes and assemblies directly from your PowerShell scripts. Given below is a guide to using .NET Framework and assemblies in PowerShell:

## Accessing .NET Classes

You can access .NET classes by using the fully qualified class name, such as [System.IO.File] for the File class in the System.IO namespace. You can call static methods directly on the class:

```
$filePath = "C:\example.txt"
$content = [System.IO.File]::ReadAllText($filePath)
Write-Output $content
```

## Creating .NET Objects

To create an instance of a .NET class, use the New-Object cmdlet or the ::new() static method:

```
# Using New-Object
$uri = New-Object -TypeName System.Uri -ArgumentList
"https://example.com"

# Using ::new()
$uri = [System.Uri]::new("https://example.com")
```

# Accessing Properties and Methods

You can access properties and methods of .NET objects just like you would with any other PowerShell object:

```
$webClient = New-Object System.Net.WebClient
$webClient.Headers.Add("User-Agent", "PowerShell")
$content = $webClient.DownloadString("https://example.com")
```

# Adding .NET Assemblies

If you want to use a .NET assembly that is not already loaded, you can use the Add-Type cmdlet to load it:

```
# Load an assembly from a file
Add-Type -Path "C:\path\to\your\assembly.dll"

# Load an assembly from GAC (Global Assembly Cache)
Add-Type -AssemblyName "System.Windows.Forms"
```

# Using .NET Assemblies

After loading an assembly, you can access its classes and methods like any other .NET classes:

```
# Load the assembly
Add-Type -AssemblyName "System.Windows.Forms"
```

```
# Create a new object from the assembly
$form = New-Object System.Windows.Forms.Form

# Set properties and call methods on the object
$form.Text = "My Form"
$form.ShowDialog()
```

# Using .NET Namespaces

To simplify your script and avoid using fully qualified class names, you can import .NET namespaces with the using namespace directive:

```
# Import a .NET namespace
using namespace System.IO

# Use the class without the fully qualified name
$fileInfo = New-Object FileInfo -ArgumentList "C:\example.txt"
```

# Creating Custom .NET Classes

You can create custom .NET classes directly in PowerShell using the Add-Type cmdlet with the -TypeDefinition parameter:

```
Add-Type -TypeDefinition @"
public class MyCustomClass {
    public static string HelloWorld() {
        return "Hello, world!";
    }
}
"@

# Use the custom class
$result = [MyCustomClass]::HelloWorld()
```

```
Write-Output $result
```

These are the basics of using the .NET Framework and assemblies in PowerShell. You can use this knowledge to incorporate .NET classes and objects into your scripts, giving you more power and flexibility.

# CHAPTER 14: POWERSHELL AND AUTOMATION FRAMEWORKS

# Introduction to Automation Frameworks

Automation frameworks are essential components in today's IT landscape, helping organizations manage their infrastructure, applications, and processes more efficiently. With the advent of cloud technologies, containerization, and microservices, automation has become more critical than ever to maintain complex and distributed systems. PowerShell is a powerful scripting language and task automation tool developed by Microsoft, designed to help automate tasks, manage configurations, and access various system components on Windows, Linux, and macOS.

Automation frameworks play a crucial role in the use of PowerShell, enabling developers, IT administrators, and DevOps engineers to create, manage, and execute scripts more effectively. These frameworks provide standardized methodologies, libraries, and tools to simplify and streamline automation tasks while increasing productivity and reducing errors. In this context, the role of automation frameworks with PowerShell can be described in the following areas:

## Script Organization and Management

Automation frameworks offer a structured approach to organizing and managing PowerShell scripts. This structure often involves using modules, functions, and cmdlets to create reusable and shareable scripts. By following a standard layout and naming conventions, administrators can easily locate, understand, and maintain their scripts, thereby reducing the complexity and improving the efficiency of the overall automation process.

## Consistency and Best Practices

Frameworks provide a set of best practices and coding standards that encourage consistency in the way PowerShell scripts are developed and maintained. By adhering to these guidelines, IT professionals can ensure that their scripts are more readable, maintainable, and scalable. Additionally, following best practices enhances security, reduces the risk of errors, and ensures that the automation process runs smoothly.

## Workflow and Process Automation

One of the essential roles of an automation framework is to support complex workflows and processes, including the automation of deployment, configuration management, and monitoring tasks. With PowerShell, these frameworks enable users to create scripts that interact with various system components, services, and applications, streamlining and automating repetitive and time-consuming tasks. PowerShell integrates with popular automation tools like Microsoft Azure Automation, AWS Systems Manager, and Chef to provide advanced workflow and process automation capabilities.

## Testing and Validation

Automation frameworks often include built-in testing and validation capabilities, ensuring that PowerShell scripts are reliable, secure, and accurate. Unit testing, integration testing, and acceptance testing can be performed using tools like Pester, a widely-used testing framework for PowerShell. By employing these testing methodologies, IT professionals can identify and fix issues early in the development process, reducing the risk of errors and improving overall automation quality.

## Continuous Integration and Continuous Deployment (CI/CD)

Automation frameworks play a significant role in enabling CI/CD pipelines with PowerShell, integrating with popular tools like Jenkins, TeamCity, and Azure DevOps. These integrations allow organizations to automate the build, test, and deployment stages of their applications, ensuring a streamlined and efficient software development lifecycle. PowerShell can be used to create scripts that interact with APIs, manage cloud resources, and configure environments, making it an integral part of modern DevOps practices.

## Cross-platform Compatibility

PowerShell Core, the open-source and cross-platform version of PowerShell, allows IT professionals to use automation frameworks across Windows, Linux, and macOS systems. This cross-platform compatibility broadens the scope of PowerShell-based automation, enabling organizations to manage heterogeneous environments more effectively. Automation frameworks that support PowerShell Core can help to ensure that scripts are compatible with multiple platforms and can be executed in diverse environments.

# PowerShell and Ansible

Integrating Ansible with PowerShell is important because it allows you to manage and automate tasks in Windows environments seamlessly. Ansible is a powerful configuration management and automation tool, while PowerShell is the preferred scripting language and shell for Windows systems. By integrating both, you can leverage the strengths of each tool and simplify the management of Windows hosts.

Given below is a step-by-step guide to integrate Ansible with PowerShell:

# Prerequisites

- Install Ansible on the control node (usually a Linux machine).
- Install and configure the Windows Subsystem for Linux (WSL) if you want to use Ansible from a Windows control node.
- Configure Windows hosts for Ansible using WinRM (Windows Remote Management) for remote access.

# Configure Ansible Inventory File

Create or edit the Ansible inventory file (usually /etc/ansible/hosts) to include your Windows hosts. Add the ansible_connection as winrm, and specify the ansible_user, ansible_password, and ansible_winrm_transport:

```
[windows]
windows-host.example.com

[windows:vars]
ansible_connection=winrm
ansible_user=Administrator
ansible_password=YourPassword
ansible_winrm_server_cert_validation=ignore
ansible_winrm_transport=ntlm
```

# Test Connection to Windows Hosts

Use the win_ping module to test the connection to your Windows hosts:

```
ansible windows -m win_ping
```

If successful, you'll receive a response like:

```
windows-host.example.com | SUCCESS => {
    "changed": false,
    "ping": "pong"
}
```

# Use PowerShell in Ansible Playbooks

You can use the win_shell module to execute PowerShell commands on Windows hosts. Create a playbook called powershell-example.yml:

```
---
- name: Execute PowerShell commands on Windows hosts
  hosts: windows
  tasks:
    - name: Get disk information
      win_shell: Get-Disk | ConvertTo-Json
      register: disk_info

    - name: Display disk information
      debug:
        var: disk_info.stdout | from_json
```

## Run the Playbook

Execute the playbook using the ansible-playbook command:

```
ansible-playbook powershell-example.yml
```

Ansible will connect to your Windows hosts, run the PowerShell command, and display the disk information.

## Use Ansible Windows Modules

Ansible provides many Windows-specific modules that use PowerShell behind the scenes. For example, the win_file module can create, delete, or modify files and directories:

```
---
- name: Manage files and directories on Windows hosts
  hosts: windows
  tasks:
    - name: Create a directory
```

```
  win_file:
    path: C:\example
    state: directory

  - name: Create a file
    win_file:
      path: C:\example\example.txt
      state: touch
```

You can find more Windows modules in the official Ansible documentation.

By integrating Ansible with PowerShell, you can manage and automate Windows environments with ease, using the powerful features of both tools.

# PowerShell and Chef

Integrating Chef with PowerShell is essential for managing and automating tasks in Windows environments efficiently. Chef is a powerful configuration management and automation tool, while PowerShell is the preferred scripting language and shell for Windows systems. By integrating both, you can leverage the strengths of each tool and streamline the management of Windows hosts.

Given below is a step-by-step guide to integrating Chef with PowerShell:

## Prerequisites

- Install Chef Workstation on your local machine (Windows, macOS, or Linux).
- Set up a Chef Server to manage your infrastructure.
- Configure your Chef Server on your Chef Workstation using the config.rb or knife.rb file.
- Bootstrap Windows nodes with the Chef Client installed and configured to communicate with the Chef Server.

## Create a Chef Cookbook

Cookbooks are the primary means to manage your infrastructure with Chef. Create a new cookbook by running the following command:

```
chef generate cookbook powershell-example
```

This command creates a new cookbook directory called powershell-example with the necessary files and structure.

## Create Recipe to Run PowerShell Commands

Recipes are Ruby files that contain resources for configuring your nodes. In the powershell-example cookbook, create a recipe file called run_powershell.rb:

```
powershell_script 'Get-DiskInfo' do
  code <<-EOH
    $diskInfo = Get-Disk | ConvertTo-Json
    Set-Content -Path 'C:\\disk_info.json' -Value $diskInfo
  EOH
end
```

This recipe uses the powershell_script resource to run a PowerShell command that retrieves disk information and saves it as a JSON file on the node.

## Add Recipe to run-list

Edit the metadata.rb file in your cookbook directory to include the new recipe:

```
name 'powershell-example'
...
version '0.1.0'
recipe 'powershell-example::run_powershell', 'Run PowerShell commands'
```

## Upload Cookbook to Chef Server

Upload the powershell-example cookbook to your Chef Server:

```
knife cookbook upload powershell-example
```

## Assign Cookbook to Windows Nodes

Assign the powershell-example::run_powershell recipe to the run-list of your Windows nodes:

```
knife node run_list add windows-node.example.com 'recipe[powershell-
example::run_powershell]'
```

## Run Chef Client on Windows Nodes

Run the Chef Client on your Windows nodes, either manually or on a schedule, to apply the powershell-example::run_powershell recipe:

```
chef-client
```

The Chef Client will execute the powershell_script resource, running the PowerShell command and saving the disk information as a JSON file.

By integrating Chef with PowerShell, you can efficiently manage and automate Windows environments, taking advantage of the powerful features of both tools.

# PowerShell and Puppet

Integrating Puppet with PowerShell is important for managing and automating tasks in Windows environments effectively. Puppet is a powerful configuration management and automation tool, while PowerShell is the preferred scripting language and shell for Windows systems. By integrating both, you can leverage the strengths of each tool and simplify the management of Windows hosts.

Given below is a step-by-step guide to integrate Puppet with PowerShell:

## Prerequisites
- Install Puppet Server to manage your infrastructure.
- Install Puppet Agent on your Windows nodes and configure them to communicate with the Puppet Server.
- Install the Puppet Development Kit (PDK) on your local machine (Windows, macOS, or Linux) to create and manage Puppet modules.

## Create Puppet Module

Modules are the primary means of managing your infrastructure with Puppet. Create a new module using the PDK:

```
pdk new module powershell_example --skip-interview
```

This command creates a new module directory called powershell_example with the necessary files and structure.

## Create Puppet Manifest to Run PowerShell Commands

Manifests are Puppet files that contain resources for configuring your nodes. In the powershell_example module, create a manifest file called run_powershell.pp in the manifests directory:

```
class powershell_example::run_powershell {
  exec { 'Get-DiskInfo':
    command => 'powershell.exe -NoProfile -ExecutionPolicy Bypass -
Command "Get-Disk | ConvertTo-Json | Set-Content -Path
\'C:\\disk_info.json\'"',
    provider => 'powershell',
  }
}
```

This manifest uses the exec resource with the powershell provider to run a PowerShell command that retrieves disk information and saves it as a JSON file on the node.

## Add Class to Main Manifest

Edit the init.pp file in the manifests directory of your module to include the new class:

```
class powershell_example {
  include powershell_example::run_powershell
}
```

## Upload Module to Puppet Server

Copy the powershell_example module to the Puppet Server's modules directory, typically found in /etc/puppetlabs/code/environments/production/modules.

## Assign Module to Windows Nodes

Assign the powershell_example class to the desired Windows nodes by including it in the appropriate node block in the Puppet Server's main manifest file, typically found in /etc/puppetlabs/code/environments/production/manifests/site.pp:

```
node 'windows-node.example.com' {
  include powershell_example
}
```

## Run Puppet Agent on Windows Nodes

Run the Puppet Agent on your Windows nodes, either manually or on a schedule, to apply the powershell_example::run_powershell class:

```
puppet agent -t
```

The Puppet Agent will execute the exec resource, running the PowerShell command and saving the disk information as a JSON file.

By integrating Puppet with PowerShell, you can efficiently manage and automate Windows environments, taking advantage of the powerful features of both tools.

# Integrating PowerShell with CI/CD Tools

Integrating CI/CD (Continuous Integration/Continuous Deployment) tools with PowerShell is important because it allows you to streamline the process of building, testing, and deploying applications in Windows environments. Jenkins is a popular open-source CI/CD tool, while PowerShell is the preferred scripting language and shell for Windows systems. By integrating Jenkins with PowerShell, you can automate tasks in your CI/CD pipeline that involve Windows hosts or require PowerShell scripts.

Given below is a step-by-step guide to integrate Jenkins with PowerShell:

## Prerequisites
- Install and configure Jenkins on a machine that can access your Windows hosts or PowerShell scripts.
- Install and configure any necessary build tools, such as Git, .NET SDK, or Visual

Studio, on the Jenkins server or build agents.

# Install PowerShell Plugin

To run PowerShell scripts in Jenkins, you need to install the PowerShell plugin:

Go to your Jenkins dashboard and navigate to "Manage Jenkins" > "Manage Plugins."

Click on the "Available" tab and search for "PowerShell."

Find the "PowerShell" plugin, check the box next to it, and click "Install without restart."

# Create Jenkins Job

Create a new Jenkins job to build, test, or deploy your application:

Go to your Jenkins dashboard and click on "New Item."

Enter a name for the job, select "Freestyle project" (or another appropriate project type), and click "OK."

Configure the job settings as needed, such as the source code repository, build triggers, and build environment.

# Add PowerShell Build Step

Add a build step in your Jenkins job to run a PowerShell script:

In the job configuration page, scroll down to the "Build" section and click "Add build step."

Select "Windows PowerShell" from the dropdown menu.

Enter your PowerShell script or the path to a PowerShell script file in the "Command" field. For example, you can use a script that compiles a .NET project:

```
cd C:\path\to\your\project
dotnet build
```

Save the job configuration.

# Run Jenkins Job

Run the Jenkins job to execute the PowerShell script in the build step.

Go to the job's main page and click "Build Now."

Monitor the progress in the "Build History" sidebar.

Click on a build number to view the build details, including the console output.

# Configure post-build Actions (optional)

You can add post-build actions to your Jenkins job to further automate the CI/CD process, such as deploying the application or sending notifications. For example, you can use a "Send files or execute commands over SSH" post-build action to deploy your application to a remote Windows host:

In the job configuration page, scroll down to the "Post-build Actions" section and click "Add post-build action."

Select "Send files or execute commands over SSH" from the dropdown menu.

Configure the SSH server, transfer settings, and remote commands as needed.

By integrating Jenkins with PowerShell, you can automate tasks in your CI/CD pipeline that involve Windows hosts or require PowerShell scripts, streamlining the process of building, testing, and deploying applications in Windows environments.

# CHAPTER 15: EXTENDING POWERSHELL AND INTEROPERABILITY

PowerShell is a powerful scripting language and automation framework designed for Windows administration, built on the .NET Framework. Its popularity stems from its flexibility, extensibility, and interoperability, which makes it an essential tool for managing Windows environments and integrating with various tools and technologies.

# Extending PowerShell

Custom Functions: Users can create custom functions in PowerShell to perform specific tasks or simplify complex operations. Functions can be written directly in the PowerShell console or saved in script files (with a .ps1 extension) for reusability. Functions can accept parameters, return values, and even process pipeline input, making them versatile and an integral part of extending PowerShell.

Modules: A module is a package containing related functions, cmdlets, variables, and other resources. Modules can be written in PowerShell or compiled in a .NET language like C#. They help organize code, simplify distribution, and promote code reuse. Users can create custom modules to extend PowerShell's functionality or install third-party modules from the PowerShell Gallery or other sources.

Custom Cmdlets: Cmdlets are specialized commands in PowerShell, usually written in a .NET language like C#. They offer better performance and more advanced functionality than PowerShell functions. Users can create custom cmdlets to extend PowerShell's capabilities, package them in modules, and distribute them for others to use.

Desired State Configuration (DSC): DSC is a management platform in PowerShell that enables users to define and enforce the desired state of their infrastructure. By extending PowerShell with DSC, users can declaratively manage Windows and Linux systems, as well as services like IIS, SQL Server, and Active Directory.

PowerShell Classes: With the introduction of PowerShell 5.0, users can define custom classes in their scripts, allowing for object-oriented programming (OOP) within PowerShell. Classes enable users to create more structured and reusable code, further extending PowerShell's capabilities.

# Interoperability

Cross-Platform Support: PowerShell Core, based on .NET Core, is a cross-platform version of PowerShell that runs on Windows, macOS, and Linux. This enables users to manage different operating systems using a single scripting language, enhancing PowerShell's interoperability.

REST APIs: PowerShell can interact with RESTful web services using the Invoke-RestMethod and Invoke-WebRequest cmdlets. This allows PowerShell to integrate with various web-based services and tools, providing a seamless way to manage and automate tasks across different platforms.

CI/CD Tools: PowerShell can be integrated with popular CI/CD tools like Jenkins, TeamCity, and Azure DevOps, enabling automation in Windows-based build, test, and deployment pipelines. This interoperability is essential for organizations that rely on Windows infrastructure and need to streamline their development processes.

Configuration Management: PowerShell can be integrated with configuration management tools like Ansible, Chef, and Puppet, allowing users to manage Windows hosts efficiently alongside other platforms. This interoperability is key to managing complex, heterogeneous environments with a single, unified toolset.

Cloud Services: PowerShell can interact with cloud platforms like AWS, Azure, and Google Cloud via their respective SDKs, modules, or APIs. This interoperability enables users to manage and automate tasks in the cloud using the same scripting language they use for on-premises infrastructure.

To sum it up, extending PowerShell and its interoperability allows users to enhance the power and reach of the scripting language. Custom functions, modules, cmdlets, and classes enable users to tailor PowerShell to their specific needs, while interoperability with various tools, technologies, and platforms ensures that PowerShell can adapt and thrive in diverse environments.

# Integrating PowerShell with Python, and Bash

Integrating PowerShell with Python and Bash enables you to leverage the capabilities of different scripting languages and run them within a single script. Given below is a guide on how to integrate PowerShell with Python and Bash:

## Integrating PowerShell with Python

Install Python on your system if it's not already installed.

Create a Python script (e.g., my_python_script.py) with your desired Python code. For example:

```python
import sys

def add_numbers(a, b):
    return a + b

if __name__ == "__main__":
    num1 = int(sys.argv[1])
    num2 = int(sys.argv[2])
    result = add_numbers(num1, num2)
    print(result)
```

In your PowerShell script, use the & operator or Start-Process cmdlet to call the Python script. Pass the path to the Python executable, followed by the path to your Python script and any required arguments:

```powershell
$pythonPath = "C:\Python39\python.exe"
$pythonScript = ".\my_python_script.py"
$num1 = 5
$num2 = 7

$result = & $pythonPath $pythonScript $num1 $num2
Write-Host "The result from the Python script is: $result"
```

## Integrating PowerShell with Bash

For this example, we'll assume you're using PowerShell Core on a Linux or macOS system, or you have Windows Subsystem for Linux (WSL) installed on your Windows machine.

Create a Bash script (e.g., my_bash_script.sh) with your desired Bash code. For example:

```bash
#!/bin/bash

function add_numbers() {
  echo $(($1 + $2))
```

```
}

num1=$1
num2=$2
result=$(add_numbers $num1 $num2)
echo $result
```

Make sure to give your script execute permissions:

```
chmod +x my_bash_script.sh
```

In your PowerShell script, use the & operator or Start-Process cmdlet to call the Bash script. Pass the path to the Bash executable (or wsl on Windows), followed by the path to your Bash script and any required arguments:

```
# If you're on Linux or macOS
$bashPath = "/bin/bash"
$bashScript = "./my_bash_script.sh"

# If you're on Windows with WSL installed
$bashPath = "wsl"
$bashScript = "/mnt/c/path/to/your/my_bash_script.sh"

$num1 = 5
$num2 = 7

$result = & $bashPath $bashScript $num1 $num2
Write-Host "The result from the Bash script is: $result"
```

By integrating PowerShell with Python and Bash, you can utilize the strengths of multiple scripting languages and perform tasks that may be more easily achieved in one language over another.

# PowerShell and RESTful APIs

PowerShell provides the Invoke-RestMethod and Invoke-WebRequest cmdlets to interact with RESTful web services. These cmdlets allow you to make HTTP requests to RESTful APIs and handle the responses.

## Invoke-RestMethod

Invoke-RestMethod simplifies the process of working with RESTful APIs by automatically converting JSON and XML responses into PowerShell objects. Given below is an example of how to use Invoke-RestMethod:

*Make an HTTP GET request:*

```
$apiUrl = "https://api.example.com/users"
$response = Invoke-RestMethod -Uri $apiUrl -Method Get
```

*Access the properties of the returned objects:*

```
foreach ($user in $response) {
    Write-Host "User ID: $($user.id)"
    Write-Host "User Name: $($user.name)"
}
```

*Make an HTTP POST request:*

```
$apiUrl = "https://api.example.com/users"
$newUser = @{
    name  = "John Doe"
    email = "john.doe@example.com"
}

$jsonBody = $newUser | ConvertTo-Json
$response = Invoke-RestMethod -Uri $apiUrl -Method Post -ContentType "application/json" -Body $jsonBody
```

# Invoke-WebRequest

Invoke-WebRequest provides more control over the HTTP request and response but requires manual parsing of the response content. Given below is an example of how to use Invoke-WebRequest:

*Make an HTTP GET request:*

```
$apiUrl = "https://api.example.com/users"
$response = Invoke-WebRequest -Uri $apiUrl -Method Get
```

*Parse the JSON response content:*

```
$parsedResponse = $response.Content | ConvertFrom-Json
```

*Access the properties of the returned objects:*

```
foreach ($user in $parsedResponse) {
    Write-Host "User ID: $($user.id)"
    Write-Host "User Name: $($user.name)"
}
```

*Make an HTTP POST request:*

```
$apiUrl = "https://api.example.com/users"
$newUser = @{
    name   = "John Doe"
    email  = "john.doe@example.com"
}
```

```
$jsonBody = $newUser | ConvertTo-Json
$response = Invoke-WebRequest -Uri $apiUrl -Method Post -ContentType
"application/json" -Body $jsonBody
```

Choose Invoke-RestMethod when you primarily need to work with JSON or XML data and prefer the automatic conversion of response content. Use Invoke-WebRequest when you need more control over the request and response or when working with non-JSON or non-XML data.

Both cmdlets support other HTTP methods like PUT, DELETE, and PATCH, as well as adding custom headers, authentication, and more. You may also look at the official documentation for more details and options available for each cmdlet.

# Creating and Consuming Web Services

In this guide, I'll demonstrate how to create a simple web service using PowerShell and then consume it using PowerShell as well.

## Create Web Service using PowerShell

We'll create a basic web service using the HttpListener class available in .NET, which allows us to create a simple HTTP server in PowerShell. For this example, we'll create a web service that receives two numbers and returns their sum.

*Create a new PowerShell script (e.g., web_service.ps1):*

```
# Load the required .NET assembly
Add-Type -AssemblyName System.Web

# Set up the HttpListener
$listener = New-Object System.Net.HttpListener
$listener.Prefixes.Add("http://localhost:8080/")
$listener.Start()

Write-Host "Listening on http://localhost:8080/"

# Main loop
while ($true) {
    $context = $listener.GetContext()
    $request = $context.Request
```

```
$response = $context.Response

# Parse query parameters
$query = [System.Web.HttpUtility]::ParseQueryString($request.Url.Query)
$number1 = [int]$query["number1"]
$number2 = [int]$query["number2"]

# Calculate the sum
$sum = $number1 + $number2

# Send the response
$buffer = [System.Text.Encoding]::UTF8.GetBytes($sum)
$response.ContentLength64 = $buffer.Length
$response.OutputStream.Write($buffer, 0, $buffer.Length)
$response.Close()
}
```

*Run the script to start the web service:*

```
.\web_service.ps1
```

The web service is now running and listening on http://localhost:8080/.

## Consume Web Service

You can consume the web service using the Invoke-RestMethod or Invoke-WebRequest cmdlets. Given below is an example using Invoke-RestMethod:

*Create a new PowerShell script (e.g., consume_web_service.ps1):*

```
$apiUrl = "http://localhost:8080"
$number1 = 5
$number2 = 7
```

```
$params = @{
    number1 = $number1
    number2 = $number2
}

# Call the web service
$response = Invoke-RestMethod -Uri $apiUrl -Method Get -Body $params

# Display the result
Write-Host "The sum of $number1 and $number2 is: $response"
```

*Run the script to consume the web service:*

```
.\consume_web_service.ps1
```

The script will make an HTTP GET request to the web service, passing the two numbers as query parameters, and the web service will return their sum.

This is a tested demonstration at my end but it is not suitable for production environments. For more robust and scalable solutions, consider using ASP.NET Core or other web frameworks to create web services, and secure them using proper authentication and authorization mechanisms.

# CHAPTER 16: WORKING WITH POWERSHELL UNIVERSAL

PowerShell Universal is a web-based platform for building, managing, and deploying PowerShell scripts, REST APIs, and web-based user interfaces. It provides a centralized platform to manage and execute PowerShell scripts and automate various tasks. PowerShell Universal is built on top of the Universal Dashboard framework, which allows you to create interactive dashboards and web applications using PowerShell.

# Why PowerShell Universal?

Cross-platform Support: PowerShell Universal supports both Windows PowerShell and PowerShell 7, which means you can run it on different platforms, including Windows, macOS, and Linux. This makes it easier to manage and automate tasks across various environments.

Centralized Management: With PowerShell Universal, you can manage all your PowerShell scripts, REST APIs, and dashboards in one place. This makes it easier to maintain, organize, and deploy your automation tasks and web applications.

Web-based Interface: The web-based interface of PowerShell Universal provides an easy-to-use platform to manage your PowerShell scripts, REST APIs, and dashboards. You can view the output of your scripts, monitor their status, schedule jobs, and manage endpoints directly from the browser, without requiring any additional software.

REST APIs: PowerShell Universal allows you to create REST APIs using PowerShell scripts easily. You can expose your PowerShell functions as RESTful web services, making it simple to integrate with other applications and services.

Role-Based Access Control (RBAC): With RBAC, you can define different access levels and permissions for your users. This ensures that users only have access to the scripts, APIs, and dashboards they need, improving security and simplifying user management.

Integrated Security: PowerShell Universal supports various authentication and authorization mechanisms, including Windows Authentication, OIDC, and OAuth 2.0. This allows you to secure your scripts, REST APIs, and dashboards using industry-standard security practices.

Scheduling: PowerShell Universal includes a built-in scheduler that allows you to schedule PowerShell scripts to run at specific intervals or times. This enables you to automate tasks without relying on external schedulers like Task Scheduler or cron.

Interactive Dashboards: Using the Universal Dashboard framework, you can create interactive, web-based dashboards and applications using PowerShell. This allows you to build custom monitoring and management tools tailored to your specific needs.

To sum it up, PowerShell Universal offers a comprehensive solution for managing and executing PowerShell scripts, creating REST APIs, and building web-based user interfaces. Its cross-platform support, centralized management, web-based interface, and integrated security make it an attractive choice for organizations looking to streamline their PowerShell automation tasks and build web applications using a familiar scripting language.

# Configure PowerShell Universal

To install and configure PowerShell Universal, follow these steps:

## Install PowerShell Universal

Download the latest version of PowerShell Universal from the official GitHub repository: https://github.com/ironmansoftware/powershell-universal/releases

Extract the contents of the downloaded ZIP file to a suitable location, e.g., C:\PowerShellUniversal.

## Configure PowerShell Universal

Open a PowerShell terminal with administrative privileges.

Navigate to the extracted PowerShell Universal folder:

```
cd C:\PowerShellUniversal
```

Start PowerShell Universal by running the following command:

```
.\Universal.Server.exe
```

This will start the PowerShell Universal server and create a default configuration file (appsettings.json) if it does not already exist.

## Access PowerShell Universal

Open a web browser and navigate to http://localhost:5000. You should see the PowerShell Universal login page.

Log in with the default username admin and password admin. It is highly recommended to change the default password after logging in for the first time.

## Configure settings

Once logged in, click on the settings icon (gear icon) in the left sidebar to access the Settings page.

Configure the desired settings, such as authentication, logging, and themes. Make sure to save your changes.

## Create Scripts, APIs, and Dashboards

In the left sidebar, click on "Automation" to manage your PowerShell scripts. You can create new scripts, view script output, and schedule scripts to run at specific intervals.

Click on "APIs" in the left sidebar to create and manage REST APIs using PowerShell scripts.

Click on "Dashboards" in the left sidebar to create and manage interactive, web-based dashboards using the Universal Dashboard framework.

## Configure PowerShell Universal as-a-Service (optional)

To ensure that PowerShell Universal starts automatically when your system boots up, you can configure it as a service. Follow these steps for Windows:

Open a PowerShell terminal with administrative privileges.

Navigate to the extracted PowerShell Universal folder:

```
cd C:\PowerShellUniversal
```

Install PowerShell Universal as a Windows service by running the following command:

```
.\install-service.ps1
```

This script installs the PowerShell Universal server as a Windows service named "PowerShellUniversal".

To start the newly installed service, run the following command:

Start-Service -Name PowerShellUniversal

For Linux and macOS, consult the official documentation to configure PowerShell Universal as a service using systemd or launchd, respectively.

Now you have PowerShell Universal installed and configured on your system. You can start managing and executing PowerShell scripts, creating REST APIs, and building web-based user interfaces using the web-based interface.

# Run scripts

Once you have installed and configured PowerShell Universal, you can run PowerShell scripts through it using the web-based interface. Given below is how to create and execute a new script:

## Create New Script

Open your web browser and go to the PowerShell Universal web interface (http://localhost:5000 by default).

Log in with your username and password.

In the left sidebar, click on "Automation".

Click the "New Script" button in the top right corner.

Enter a name for the new script (e.g., "MyScript.ps1").

Click "Create" to create the new script.

## Edit the Script

In the "Automation" section, click on the script you just created (e.g., "MyScript.ps1").

You'll be redirected to the script editor. Here, you can enter your PowerShell script code. For example:

$currentTime = Get-Date

```
Write-Output "The current time is: $currentTime"
```

Click "Save" in the top right corner to save your changes.

## Run the Script

In the script editor, click the "Run" button in the top right corner to execute the script.

After the script finishes running, you'll see the output in the "Output" tab below the script editor.

## View Script Hstory and Output

In the left sidebar, click on "Automation".

Click on the script you want to view the history for (e.g., "MyScript.ps1").

In the "History" tab below the script editor, you can see a list of all the script executions.

Click on an execution to view the script output, error messages, and other details.

Now you know how to create, edit, and run PowerShell scripts using the PowerShell Universal web interface. You can also schedule scripts to run automatically at specific intervals, view the execution history, and manage multiple scripts from the "Automation" section.

# Powershell scheduling

In PowerShell Universal, you can schedule scripts to run at specific intervals or times using the built-in scheduler. Given below is how to create a new scheduled job for a script:

## Create a New Schedule

Open your web browser and go to the PowerShell Universal web interface (http://localhost:5000 by default).

Log in with your username and password.

In the left sidebar, click on "Automation".

Click on the "Schedules" tab located near the top of the page.

Click the "New Schedule" button in the top right corner.

Enter a name for the new schedule (e.g., "MySchedule").

In the "Cron Expression" field, enter a cron expression that defines the schedule's frequency. A cron expression is a string representing a schedule in the format * * * * *, where each field (from left to right) represents minutes, hours, days of the month, months, and days of the week, respectively. For example:

* * * * *: Run every minute.
0 * * * *: Run every hour at the top of the hour.
0 0 * * *: Run every day at midnight.

You can use a tool like CronTab Guru to generate cron expressions.

Click "Create" to create the new schedule.

## Assign Script to Schedule

In the "Schedules" tab, click on the schedule you just created (e.g., "MySchedule").

In the "Scripts" field, start typing the name of the script you want to assign to the schedule, and select it from the autocomplete suggestions (e.g., "MyScript.ps1").

Click "Save" in the top right corner to save your changes.

Now, the specified script will run according to the schedule you defined. You can view the script execution history and output by navigating to the script in the "Automation" section and clicking on the "History" tab. To edit or delete a schedule, go to the "Schedules" tab in the "Automation" section, click on the schedule you want to modify, and use the "Edit" or "Delete" buttons in the top right corner. You can create multiple schedules and assign different scripts to them as needed. This allows you to automate various tasks and run scripts at specific intervals or times without relying on external schedulers like Task Scheduler or cron.

Overall, PowerShell Universal is a web-based platform for building, managing, and deploying PowerShell scripts, REST APIs, and web-based user interfaces. It supports both Windows PowerShell and PowerShell 7, making it cross-platform compatible with

Windows, macOS, and Linux. With PowerShell Universal, you can centrally manage all your PowerShell scripts, REST APIs, and interactive dashboards, and execute them through a web-based interface.

Installing and configuring PowerShell Universal is straightforward. download the latest version from the official GitHub repository, extract the contents, and start the Universal.Server.exe. Optionally, you can configure it as a service to start automatically during system boot.

PowerShell Universal offers role-based access control for managing user permissions and supports various authentication and authorization mechanisms. Its built-in scheduler enables you to run scripts at specific intervals or times without relying on external schedulers.

Using the web interface, you can create and execute PowerShell scripts, view their output, and manage their schedules. You can also create REST APIs using PowerShell scripts and build interactive, web-based dashboards using the Universal Dashboard framework.

PowerShell Universal is a comprehensive solution for managing and executing PowerShell scripts, creating REST APIs, and building web-based user interfaces. Its cross-platform support, centralized management, web-based interface, and integrated security make it a powerful tool for organizations looking to streamline their PowerShell automation tasks and build web applications using a familiar scripting language.

# Thank You

# Epilogue

This comprehensive guide offers readers a deep dive into the world of PowerShell and how to use it effectively in system administration.

As businesses continue to rely heavily on technology, there is a growing demand for skilled IT professionals who can efficiently manage complex systems. PowerShell has emerged as a powerful tool for automating various administrative tasks, reducing human error, and improving productivity. Your book is a valuable resource for both novice and experienced system administrators, providing them with a solid understanding of PowerShell and how it can be used to streamline their workflows.

The book covers all aspects of PowerShell, from basic concepts and syntax to advanced topics such as creating custom modules, integrating with other languages, and building web-based user interfaces. It also provides practical examples and real-world scenarios to help readers apply their knowledge in real-world situations.

One of the unique features of your book is its emphasis on hands-on learning. Throughout the book, readers are encouraged to follow along with the examples and exercises provided, enabling them to gain practical experience and reinforce their understanding of PowerShell. Additionally, your book offers numerous tips and best practices to help readers optimize their PowerShell scripts and achieve better results.

By reading PowerShell SysAdmin Crash Course, readers will gain a deep understanding of PowerShell and how to use it effectively in system administration. They will be equipped with the tools and knowledge necessary to automate various administrative tasks, reduce human error, and improve productivity. This book is an invaluable resource for anyone seeking to master PowerShell and advance their career in IT.